THE ESSENTIALS
Providing High-Quality Family Child Care

THE ESSENTIALS
Providing High-Quality Family Child Care

Marie L. Masterson and Lisa M. Ginet

National Association for the Education of Young Children
Washington, DC

National Association for the
Education of Young Children
1401 H Street NW, Suite 600
Washington, DC 20005
202-232-8777 • 800-424-2460
NAEYC.org

NAEYC Books

Senior Director, Publishing and
Professional Learning
Susan Friedman

Editor in Chief
Kathy Charner

Senior Creative Design Manager
Audra Meckstroth

Senior Editor
Holly Bohart

Publishing Manager
Francine Markowitz

Creative Designer
Malini Dominey

Associate Editor
Rossella Procopio

Through its publications program,
the National Association for the
Education of Young Children
(NAEYC) provides a forum for
discussion of major issues and
ideas in the early childhood
field, with the hope of provoking
thought and promoting
professional growth. The views
expressed or implied in this book
are not necessarily those of the
Association.

Photo Credits

Copyright © NAEYC: 22 and 53

Copyright © Vera Wiest: 63

Copyright © Getty Images: viii, 5 (both), 9, 13 (both), 17 (both),
21 (both), 27, 33, 37 (both), 41, 45, 48, 55, 59 (both), and 66

Library of Congress Control Number: 2018935988

ISBN: 978-1-938113-35-2

Item 1135

Contents

Foreword

The young family child care provider standing in front of me at a conference in Mobile, Alabama, is bursting with energy. She clearly loves caring for the children in her home and supporting their families as a partner in their children's early education. With a great deal of enthusiasm, she describes how she's also become very interested in the business side of family child care. She's worked hard to learn more, and now she's sharing her expertise with other family child care providers so they too can have more successful businesses. Beyond that, she has become actively engaged with her state association for family child care providers and is interested in working at the national level.

As CEO for the National Association for Family Child Care (NAFCC), I have the privilege of meeting family child care providers from around the country. The meeting in Mobile is a perfect example of the wonderful and unique opportunities that are part of being a family child care business owner. No other part of the early care and education field offers the opportunity to run your own business from home, have a profound impact on the lives of children and their families, and become a leader within your field at the local, state, or national level.

Many people focus on the word *care* in family child care. But if you look closer, you'll see a career opportunity that is deeply rewarding on many levels. Family child care providers, or *providers* as they are often called, are quick to tell you that it is all about "their kids" and the families they serve. But family child care is about more than just helping children build the foundations of their lives. At the end of the day, it is still a business, one in which you are the boss. Your success is determined by your own hard work and commitment to quality. As with the young woman I met in Mobile, you are limited only by your dreams and willingness to work toward them.

Whether you are a new family child care provider just starting out, or someone who's been in business for a while, you will find *The Essentials: Providing High-Quality Family Child Care* to be a valuable roadmap on your journey to build your own successful family child care business. The authors, Marie Masterson and Lisa Ginet, are experts from two of our field's strongest supporters of family child care, the McCormick Center for Early Childhood Leadership and Erikson Institute. The authors recognize that one book cannot contain all you need to know to build a high-quality family child care business, so they have also filled these pages with great references to other publications and organizations that you will find useful on your journey.

And I do mean journey. Your business is about creating a high-quality learning environment for the children in your care. Your work will have a profound impact on their lives and the lives of their children as well. Throughout your career as a family child care provider, you'll be inspired to continually look for ways to create new learning opportunities for the children, find new ways to support their families, and discover new ways to improve your own bottom line.

Please accept a huge thank-you for joining the ranks of family child care business owners! It is an amazing field of opportunity that has enormous importance to our society. Thanks also to the authors for writing a much-needed contribution to the literature on starting and running a family child care business. Finally, thank you to CEO Rhian Evans Allvin and her team at NAEYC for their ongoing partnership with NAFCC to support family child care providers across the nation.

—Bill Hudson
Chief Executive Officer,
National Association for Family Child Care

About the Book

Family child care is a vital part of early childhood education. According to the National Association for Family Child Care (NAFCC), there are nearly 3 million children in family child care (NAFCC 2018a). Many enter as infants or toddlers. Preschoolers may be in family child care exclusively or in addition to attending a child care center or school-based program. Families who have children in early elementary school may use family child care during holidays, school breaks, and before and after the regular school day.

The information and guidance in this book support the efforts of family child care providers to use effective, responsive practices to offer high-quality care and education for children.

This Book Is for You!

This guide, which is part of The Essentials series, provides a brief introduction to the family child care profession. Whether you are new to family child care or have years of experience, this book is for you. It includes

- » Tips and strategies to help you develop and manage a well-organized business
- » Ways to maximize dual-use spaces and enhance your materials and routines
- » Guidelines and tips to help you balance your home and professional needs
- » Examples of effective, responsive practices to help you adapt to the unique needs of each child in your program
- » Support and information in stories that are labeled "Voice of family child care"
- » Reflections and suggestions from family child care providers
- » Practical information to help you build positive and meaningful relationships with families

Each section includes a variety of resources that you can use to expand your knowledge and skills to help you continue to meet the needs of children and families and support a high-quality family child care experience.

What You Will Find in this Book

Chapter 1, "What Is Family Child Care?," defines family child care, explains its value, and outlines its advantages, emphasizing how to work with families to meet the individual strengths, abilities, and skills of every child.

Chapter 2, "Building Your Family Child Care Business," addresses licensing regulations, business policies, and setting policies.

Chapter 3, "Learning Spaces in Family Child Care," includes information about dual-use spaces, setting up an environment that supports children's learning, and selecting learning materials.

Chapter 4, "Teaching in High-Quality Family Child Care," describes the importance of routines and schedules, strengths-based observation, and positive guidance.

Chapter 5, "Professional and Program Growth," describes accreditation, quality rating and improvement systems (QRIS), and professional learning resources.

1 What Is Family Child Care?

Marianna was a health care aide for six years before starting a family. When her own daughter turns 3, Marianna begins taking care of her neighbor's infant daughter during the day. Soon other friends ask her to watch their children. It isn't long before she decides to plan for and open a licensed family child care business. She learns a lot by joining a community family child care group that meets once a month. "I wish I had known sooner that I could run a business like this from my home. I enjoy working with families and helping children learn. And I get to stay home with my daughter!"

Like others in family child care, Marianna enjoys her work. She knows how children develop and learn, and she enjoys teaching them. The children's families are grateful because they know their children are learning in a safe, supportive environment. Marianna knows that they appreciate finding high-quality family child care in their neighborhood.

The National Association of Family Child Care (NAFCC) defines *family child care* as the business of child care and the practice of early care and education in the program provider's home (NAFCC 2018a). On average, family child care educators care for and educate about eight children a week (NSECE 2016). Most family child care homes have one adult educator. The size of the group of children is set by the state. Forty-six states limit that number to six children, nine states permit 10 or more children, and all states set limits on the number of infants and toddlers. In 41 states, the number of children includes the educator's own children (NCCCQI & NARA 2015). The number of hours that children spend in the home varies. Arrangements are often flexible for children and more affordable for families than those in other settings. Children may spend part of the day in a child care center or school, another part in a family child care home, and the evening with a grandmother or other family member. Family child care homes are an essential part of child care that children and their families need.

Sixty percent of children from birth to age 5 who are not yet in kindergarten are in some type of nonparental care (Redford, Desrochers, & Mulvaney Hoyer 2017). Family child care is the most prevalent child care arrangement for these children (Porter & Bromer 2017). There are more than 129,000 licensed family child care homes in the United States (NCCCQI & NARA 2015). NAFCC (2018a) reports that of 11 million children under age 5 in child care, nearly 3 million are in family child care, with approximately 1 million paid providers.

Family child care is an important resource for families with children in preschool. Forty-four percent of employed mothers and 41 percent of non-employed mothers use multiple child care arrangements that include a family child care setting. Preschoolers whose mothers work spend the most hours in family child care settings, around 33 hours a week (Laughlin 2013). They are more likely than younger children to spend extended time in a nonparental setting (Redford, Desrochers, & Mulvaney Hoyer 2017).

While the federal government sets guidelines for safety and health, states independently establish specific standards for licensing family child care businesses (Child Care Aware of America 2018a). States set minimum standards for the basic components of family child care, including adult-to-child ratio, group size, and the level of education and training that is required. State and local regulations include fire codes, vaccination requirements, and food-handling guidelines. These minimum standards provide an important safeguard for children. Families look for licensed child care for their children because they expect that it will provide a basic level of health and safety for their children.

In addition to following state and local regulations and licensing rules and standards, there are other ways to develop a high-quality family child care program. NAFCC offers a national accreditation program that is designed to help family child care educators "achieve a high level of quality through a process that examines all aspects of the family child care program" (NAFCC 2018b). In addition, the National Association for the Education of Young Children (NAEYC) provides important guidelines for developmentally appropriate and culturally responsive practice. The information in NAEYC's position statements (NAEYC.org/resources/position-statements) represent high-quality guidance and support for teaching young children. In addition, the NAEYC Code of Ethical Conduct offers guidance for addressing and resolving challenging situations with children, families, colleagues, and the community.

A unique feature of family child care is that children often stay for a number of years. Children may begin with your program when they are infants or toddlers and continue coming after school, during the summer, or on some holidays until they are in kindergarten or first or second grade. Over the years, you develop close relationships with children and get to know their families well, which adds to your ability to know how their children learn best. This gives you the opportunity to make a difference in their lives.

Most important to the success of your family child care program are your unique strengths. You are the key to children's positive experiences. Your knowledge, skills, and interests and your unique personality and passions influence the quality of your program, including daily interactions with children and families. The joy you bring to teaching, your love of reading, your curiosity, and your teaching skills affect how children learn. Your interpersonal skills and organizational abilities—and the value you place on your own health and well-being—will help you run your business smoothly. Most important, children and their families benefit from your dedication to high quality and your commitment to children's learning and development.

Because you support children as they develop the knowledge, skills, and understanding they need, you have the opportunity to have a life-changing impact on the lives of children and families.

A Day in Family Child Care

Logan and Mia happily rush to Francesca's front door, anticipating spending time at Francesca's family child care program. Their mom sees how happy Logan and Mia are to greet the other children. Francesca smiles and pets the long ears on Logan's bunny, Floppy. When she asks if the children are hungry, Logan wants to know if Floppy can eat with them. "Of course he can," laughs Francesca.

Three-year-old Rachel arrived before Logan and Mia. She sits next to them as their mom reads *Chicka Chicka Boom Boom* before saying goodbye. The children are busy putting together puzzles by the time their mom leaves for work.

Each day, Francesca plans mealtimes and other routines based on the developmental needs of the eight children who will be present. The families of two children speak Spanish in their home, and today's plans include baking *galletas* (cookies). While they are making the galletas, she talks with the children about how they help their families cook. Afterwards, they pretend they are going to *la panadería* (the bakery) to buy *pasteles* (pastries) and galletas. The children learn at their own pace through daily interactions, routines, and planned activities. Because Francesca knows each child well, she understands that their day-to-day needs and interests may change. The children at her family child care home enjoy being in a program that supports their learning and development.

Family child care is not a mini-classroom. Many activities and routines that are part of school- and center-based settings are designed for large groups of children. The intimate small group setting of family child care allows you to do things differently and to take advantage of a unique setting and your skills and resources. You can invite children to enjoy your hobbies, such as sewing, crafting, model building, or music. You can select books and activities that match their unique interests and allow extended time for them to pursue projects deeply.

The more you know about how children grow and change through the early years, the more you are able to pay attention to and respond to their needs (Bueno, Darling-Hammond, & Gonzales 2010). To ensure a happy and successful experience for each child, family child care educators

- » Become highly skilled in using positive behavior guidance
- » Know how to encourage and build on children's strengths
- » Discover creative ways to challenge and support children's growing abilities
- » Learn to read children's signs and cues that show how they are feeling and when they need encouragement or a change of pace

Your daily schedule includes pleasant conversation and friendly mealtime interactions. Children have extended time for play and learning, like they might have at their own home. They may engage in dramatic play, creating their own scenarios. They may dress up, act out roles, or create imaginative stories with props such as stuffed animals, cardboard tubes, or goggles. They may imitate what they see at home and in their communities. The materials, toys, and other supplies that you make available for the children reflect their interests and the teaching plans you have for them.

As you interact with children throughout the day, they learn new words when you share a recipe or look at leaves or insects outside. When you read books and tell stories with interest and enthusiasm, they understand that reading is important and enjoyable. During the day, the children may notice a problem and then work with you to solve it. For example, they need additional space to build puzzles and decide to use cookie sheets to move their work from the coffee table to the dining room table. They learn to make decisions throughout daily activities.

Throughout the day, you notice what each child knows and understands. You use this insight to plan interesting and engaging activities for each child to boost her learning. For example, for a child who loves to paint, you offer different interesting materials to paint such as boxes, paper plates, or textured papers. When a child enjoys working in the garden, you help him learn to prune and water indoor plants. When you follow children's interests, you foster engaged learning.

You celebrate birthdays and delight in an infant's first steps and in the joy of each child learning and developing new skills. Sharing the details of each day with the children's families helps them feel connected to the experiences their children have in your family child care home.

Interactions Matter

Throughout the day, as you laugh with the children and have serious conversations with them, your interactions communicate that you care about them. The warm and caring relationships you help children develop with each other are just as important as the one they have with you. Like with siblings, you help the children get along and learn to appreciate and cooperate with each other. With your guidance and support, they develop the social and emotional skills that they need, so they are able to express their own feelings and listen to and respect others' ideas and feelings. Throughout the day—while children are talking, playing, listening to music, taking a walk in the neighborhood, and enjoying the other activities you planned—they are practicing the skills they need to establish and sustain warm, caring, and healthy relationships that will help them be successful in school and in life.

You observe each child and learn their personality and temperament. When you notice that a child's behavior seems different than it usually is, you respond to this change. For some children, that means teaching them strategies for calming. Others might need quiet activities to refocus their energy, while some need support to join in other children's play. You may notice they are interested in books on a certain topic, such as trains or bugs, or they might be ready for an additional challenge with fine motor or math activities. Your responsiveness ensures that their needs are met and that they are continuing to learn.

Rich conversations that use back-and-forth, serve-and-return interactions strengthen children's emotional connection and language ability (Head Zauche et al. 2016; Vallotton & Ayoub 2011). Language skills help them learn to express themselves and understand both their own and other children's emotions (Cohen 2010; Girard et al. 2016). These abilities help them make friends and get along with others. These positive social and emotional experiences build on each other, resulting in a strong foundation for future learning (Denham & Brown 2010).

When you are patient during daily routines, you support children's sense of worth. When you keep routines and schedules predictable, children know what is expected and can anticipate what is coming next. This creates a low-stress, high-nurturing environment where children's social, emotional, cognitive, and physical needs are met in safe and healthy ways that nurture their learning, growth, and development.

The Benefits of Family Child Care

On the last day before spring break, Blaire gives Tessa and Hudson a goodbye hug. "Have a happy trip! Take pictures for me. I will miss you, and I can't wait to see you again!" Over the break, the children will be traveling with their family. Kayla Martin, Tessa and Hudson's mom, thanks Blaire for keeping Tessa and Hudson an extra hour that day so she had time to run errands. Kayla says, "We want you to know how much we appreciate all you are doing to teach Tessa and Hudson. It's a relief to know how much they enjoy being with you and the other children." Blaire hugs Kayla, too. "I look forward to seeing all of you when you get back."

Like Blaire, you value the relationships you have with children and their families. You may have had an experience like the following:

Voice of family child care—I enjoy supporting children *and* families. I am invested in their children, something that matters to me and to them. I can address issues effectively and quickly because I have established relationships with the children's families and use ongoing communication to receive feedback from them. When challenging situations come up, I rely on the relationships I have with families. I often ask them for their ideas and suggestions so we can work together to find a solution.

Many families prefer family child care because such an arrangement provides a consistent caregiver, a group of tight-knit families, flexible hours and days of care, and mixed-age groupings (Harper Browne 2009). When you work together with families, the benefits of that coordinated care include the following:

A strong home–caregiver partnership. The partnership you build with families is one of many distinct benefits of family child care. You have the opportunity to get to know parents and other family members well. Over time, you may care for children and their siblings. This long-term relationship provides stability and consistency for children and their families.

Culturally responsive practice. A family's language, culture, values, and community connections are part of their family life and influence how they raise their children, including

- » How they support their child's independence and social interactions
- » How children express emotions and ask for help
- » How families nurture, calm, or comfort their children
- » How they prepare and eat meals
- » How families respond to illness
- » How families communicate

The more you know and honor a family's values, culture, and priorities, the easier it is to work with them to educate and care for their child. Talk with parents about what they expect. It is important to honor and respect a family's language, culture, and customs in order to create an environment that feels familiar and comfortable for both the children and their families. Over time, you will learn ways to reflect and promote the cultural practices of children's families and be intentional about creating an open and inviting space as you build on the unique cultural strengths of the children's families and the community (Farinde-Wu, Glover, & Williams 2017).

Extended family networks. Parents often choose family child care because they want their children's learning experiences to be like a home away from home (CCRS 2009). When you know and interact with families over a number of years, you can form lifelong friendships and ongoing support systems (King 2012).

A nurturing environment for infants and toddlers. Families who have infants and toddlers often choose family child care programs because of their smaller group settings so that their children receive individual attention and caring interactions. The lower child–teacher ratio in family child care provides many opportunities for close relationships among children, families, and you. You give infants and toddlers (and other children too!) a strong, secure foundation for their learning and development by providing well-coordinated care.

The Foundations of High-Quality Family Child Care

Four-year-olds Cecil and Tyler love to play with the magnetic tiles, to the exclusion of everything else. Today, they are making castles. "I have the tallest turret going up from the walkway," Cecil says, showing the other children. "I am making a moat and cross bridge," adds Tyler. Greta supports their interest in knights and castles by reading books to them about this topic and creating a basket of materials that they can use with the castles they build. Cecil and Tyler buried a "treasure" outside and are playing "find the treasure" by giving clues to where the treasure is located and telling some children when they are "hot" (near the treasure) or "cold" (far away from the treasure) to help them find it. Although the ground is covered in snow, the children carry out their play by stomping the snow down with their boots.

Greta reads the castle books with enthusiasm, knowing that she is encouraging the children's learning. She matches the activities she plans to the children's interests and strengths. Whether they want to know more about nature, cooking, castles, or cars, she enjoys helping them find information and materials.

In the same way, you use the unique resources of your home, outdoor area, and community to support children's interests and extend their learning. If you have older children, they may focus on their hobbies or on the subjects they are learning in school. If you have younger children, their interests may change over time as they have new experiences. As a result, no two family child care homes share an identical schedule or approach. Nevertheless, there are some shared basics of family child care practice that are foundational to high-quality care.

The most important goal is to nurture children's learning and development and to work with the children's families to ensure the highest-quality care. You look for ways to understand each child's unique needs. You guide all of the goals and practices of your family child care setting through your commitment to supporting the children's learning and development.

Effective Communication

> **Voice of family child care**—I learned that if a requirement is not written clearly in the handbook, I can't enforce it. I like to help families. I also want them to appreciate what I am doing. At first, I let children stay extra minutes without charging. I didn't know how to turn that around and enforce the rule. I waited until the middle of December. Then I sent home a note that said, "While I understand your work schedules and want to help, beginning January 1, I will be enforcing the handbook guidelines about pickup times." Everyone started coming on time—or offering to pay the fee. I wish I had done that sooner.

Parents want to know that their child will be safe and happy in the family child care program they choose. They want to understand what is expected of them. What will their children do each day? What will happen if they are late? The following guidelines can help you talk with families clearly about the way you care for children and provide common language to discuss important issues.

Keep policies and schedules visible. Families appreciate it when policies and communication are well stated and clear in a handbook or on your website. Post emergency contact information for fire and police departments and display local health and safety regulations. Put daily schedules, mealtimes, and sleep schedules where families can see them. (See "Setting Policies," pages 15–18, for more information.)

Foster open communication. Invite families to ask questions about schedules, plans, and activities. Give or send home daily reports of when children sleep, what and when they eat, and the planned play activities for younger children. Ask families to offer suggestions for activities, games, and books that they know their children will enjoy.

Use child-centered routines. Remind families that your goal is to provide child-centered care. Explain that meals will be family style and that you take a positive approach to children's self-care routines so every child feels safe and nurtured. Tell families that you encourage children to talk about their ideas and have conversations with other children and that your curriculum plans are flexible, allowing the children to choose how they want to play.

Plan for balanced activity. Communicate your commitment to the health and well-being of each child, which includes daily outdoor large muscle activities such as jumping, climbing, and running. Encourage the children to play games and activities with each other while also ensuring there is space for quiet play with time to pursue individual interests and flexible time for rest and relaxation.

Use a whole-child approach. Because you know that development in one area is often related to development in other areas, you plan activities and experiences that support development in many areas. For example, encourage children to independently explore materials, as this supports both their cognitive development *and* their small muscle development. Encourage children's interests by reading a variety of age-appropriate books and materials to them and letting them explore the books independently. The caring conversations you have with the children are designed to support their social and language development.

Ensure age-appropriate technology. When you use a digital tool, you make sure that it is age appropriate. You have a clearly stated policy in your handbook so families know that your plans for children include limited and purposeful use of technology. You use the guidelines of the American Academy of Pediatrics and the joint position statement from NAEYC and the Fred Rogers Center (located at NAEYC.org) when choosing technology and media for your program.

Create a positive climate. Each day, you make sure that children feel safe to contribute and share their ideas. You protect each child's emotional and physical safety, making sure they feel secure and supported. You recognize that over time, children develop self-regulation and social skills with the help and support of caring adults.

Summary

As a family child care educator, you have the unique opportunity to foster children's development and learning. You use your unique traits and training to create meaningful routines, activities, and learning experiences for children. Children feel secure and enjoy a positive relationship with you and with each other. Families appreciate your commitment to them and feel confident that their children are thriving in a high-quality setting. As you develop each element of your program, you discover many opportunities to grow as a professional and develop your strengths. You take pride in knowing that what you offer families and children meets an important need and makes a positive difference.

2 Building Your Family Child Care Business

Voice of family child care—I knew family child care was an important option for families. I really wanted to work with children using my knowledge and abilities and to work from home. I decided to figure out what I needed to do to open a family child care business. First, I made sure my family was supportive. Then, I made sure my home was a safe environment to care for children. That included many things, including having my fence fixed, something I needed to do anyway. Most important, a current family child care educator promised to guide and help me while I adapted my home to meet licensing regulations. I knew that was an important step to take so I could open and operate a successful family child care business.

Understanding Licensing Regulations

Complying with licensing regulations is an important early step to launching and maintaining your family child care business. The licensing regulations in each state ensure the health and safety of children. To own and operate your business, you must know and follow local and state licensing regulations. While child care licensing standards set the minimum acceptable health, safety, and program standards for the legal operation of programs, compliance itself is not an indicator of quality care. State licensing is a baseline of regulated care, below which it is illegal to operate (Child Care Aware of America 2018).

By following licensing regulations, you ensure that your home is ready and safe for children. Complying with the regulations includes compiling documentation related to health and safety, including adult–child ratios, emergency contacts, and insurance information. In many states, you need to

» Keep certain information in a secure place, including child information cards, immunizations, medication and dosage records, and transportation permissions.

» Have a plan for fire, safety, and tornado drills, and keep certain first aid supplies on hand.

» Have up-to-date training and certification records, including background checks and current cardiopulmonary resuscitation (CPR) and first aid certificates.

» Certify that you have sudden infant death syndrome (SIDS) training.

A licensing specialist will evaluate your physical environment to make sure it meets all safety and health standards for the number of children who will be in your home. Some of the things a specialist evaluates include

» Adequate physical space

» Safe lighting and heating

» Safe storage of all hazardous materials

In addition, all pets in your home need to be vaccinated and all weapons licensed and properly secured.

The regulations apply to all areas of your house where children will be present to ensure their safety in spaces such as the bathroom, diapering areas, and rooms where they play or sleep. Licensing regulations provide basic guidelines for safe food preparation and storage areas and for proper sanitation and cleaning. Indoor protections include covered electrical outlets and other safety precautions. Outside, you will need play areas with proper fencing. You should also ensure that the part of your home that children walk through to go from inside play to outside play is safe and hazard free.

There are more than 400 local child care resource and referral agencies across the United States that can help you with resources (visit www.childcareaware.org/ccrr-search-form to search the locations of these agencies). Child Care Aware of America's website (www.childcareaware.org) can also help you find business development tips, health and safety resources, child care fact sheets, and detailed licensing information on an interactive state map.

Managing Your Business

Voice of family child care—It sounds cliché, but setting things out the night before has really helped me be ready for the next day. I need to get my son off to school around the time the children arrive, so having his lunch prepared and papers signed before I go to sleep makes it possible for me to spend time with him the next morning. Knowing he leaves for school happy and ready for the day is an enormous boost to my own day.

You juggle many responsibilities. In addition to being the primary caregiver and educator for children, you play many roles—including nutritionist, first aid provider, and business owner—all in your home. To successfully carry out these complex duties, you must organize

your time, space, and materials strategically. In addition, you need to set aside time to manage your business and financial responsibilities.

It helps to organize your week using a calendar, wall organizer, to-do lists, and schedule. Not only will you keep track of what needs to be done each day, you will also keep a record that can help you become more realistic about how to manage your many responsibilities.

> **Voice of family child care**—I know I should log in my receipts regularly. To be honest, the first year, I just threw them in a drawer, and I had to figure it all out at the end of the year. The following year I totaled them each month and kept better notes. I know some people take care of records weekly. I now keep all of my records together and write a brief description of items I purchase on the back of the receipt before I place it in the file. Keeping accurate records has helped me become better at managing my business.

Record Keeping

Schedule a regular time to keep your records up to date. Set aside a convenient physical space for records and documents that is separate from your personal files. Clearly label folders and keep them in bins or file drawers along with any appropriate digital records. Setting aside a well-defined space for your computer and office equipment makes record keeping, ordering, and communication easier.

Store your receipts in a secure place or use online software such as QuickBooks, KidKare, or a record-keeping calendar. Make sure you store all files related to your business—including financial information—in a locked cabinet or other place that is not accessible to others. Likewise, store digital files in a password-protected location on your computer or other device.

Record keeping includes tracking both your income and expenses. Income includes all money received from families, including tuition, late fees, and registration fees; money from your state's child care subsidy program; reimbursements from the Child and Adult Care Food Program; and money from any other source, including grants. Keep accurate records so that you know how much money you receive from each source.

For tax purposes, keep track of all expenses directly associated with your family child care business, such as toys, classroom materials (like art supplies, books, and math manipulatives), playground equipment, food, highchairs, cubbies, children's furniture, and training and professional development workshops and classes. Check tax regulations about deducting a portion of your home expenses, including property tax, mortgage interest, rent, utilities, house insurance, house repairs, and house depreciation. You may also be able to deduct a portion of household items such as cleaning supplies, light bulbs, toilet paper, paper towels, and kitchen supplies. If your curriculum plans include a field trip to a local park, children's museum, or other learning experience and you use your car to take children to these places, you may be able to deduct expenses connected to these trips and costs for using your car or van for business trips to the bank, grocery store, or other places. (*Note:* If you use your vehicle to transport children, make sure that your insurance covers this use.)

Consider attending a training session or scheduling a consultation with a tax specialist who understands and works regularly with family child care business owners to understand what you can deduct and the financial receipts and records you need to keep. A professional review by a tax accountant can provide accurate information about tax preparation for your unique circumstances. Ask other family child care educators to recommend a tax professional who they feel does a good job. A few guidelines to stay organized include:

- » Save receipts for everything associated with cleaning, repairing, and maintaining your home. If you are not sure whether an item you buy is tax deductible (for example, rug shampoo, towels, or grass seed), save the receipt anyway.

- » Keep a daily record of all the meals and snacks you serve to the children in your program. This includes those reimbursed by a food program and any other meals or snacks you serve. Food not reimbursed by a food program may still be deductible on your taxes. These deductions add up. If you regularly serve an afternoon snack that is not reimbursed, it can represent a sizable business deduction.

- » Keep a daily record for at least two months each year to document the hours you work in your home on business activities. This includes the hours you are with children and those spent on business activities when children are not in your home. Business activities include cleaning the rooms in your home where children play, learn, and are cared for; planning curriculum; keeping records; and talking with families on the phone or sending them emails. The number of hours you work may determine how much of your home expenses you can deduct.

» Review your records at least once a month to make sure you have kept everything you should. If you lost or did not receive a receipt, you can re-create it by writing down what you bought, when you bought it, and how much it cost. You can document the purchase by taking a photo of the item and attaching the photo to the documentation. Save all business records for at least three years. Check the rules for your state, as you may need to keep the records longer than three years where you live.

Record keeping gets easier with practice. Don't worry if you do not master everything right away. Over time, you will get better at record keeping.

Insurance

In addition to record keeping, make sure you have protected yourself—as well as your home, family, children, vehicle, pets, and property—from the risks of running a family child care business in your home. Start by asking your insurance agent if your current policy covers all aspects of your family child care business. Some policies do, but others do not. Ask for a written statement of what is covered. In addition, purchase business liability insurance to protect yourself from potential lawsuits and if a child or a child's family member is injured.

Marketing

Although many families find child care through word of mouth, you will need to market your family child care business. If you are just getting started, join your local family child care association and ask other providers for advice. Talk to your local child care resource and referral agency about how to promote your program. If your business is established, offer parents a finder's fee or a discount for referrals to your program. Be sure that your rates are set to match the typical fees of similar quality programs in your area.

Over time, you will develop strong business skills and discover what works best in your area. Your ability to manage your business and stay organized will reduce the time you spend running your business. Connect with local people and resources that can help you make your business more efficient so you can spend more time enjoying and teaching the children in your care.

Setting Policies

In addition to making decisions about organizing your time, space, and records, you need to develop written policies to make sure families understand your expectations.

Contract

While no two businesses are identical, a contract that outlines written expectations sets boundaries for your time and makes sure that you are paid for your work. Talking with a lawyer about a contract is a good idea. Most contracts include the following elements:

1. The name of the parent(s) or other significant adult(s) in the child's life, the child(ren)'s name(s), and your name.

2. The days and/or hours your business is open and the date you will begin caring for the child(ren).

3. The amount of money the family must pay for your services. Establish a daily, weekly, or monthly rate.

4. Fees for additional services, such as registration fees, late pickup fees, or field trip fees.

5. Information about holidays, your vacation time, sick days, and rates during children's absences.

6. Notice of how the contract will end. Typically, families are required to give a two-week notice to terminate the contract. Be sure to state that payment is due for the two-week period, even if the family withdraws their child sooner. Also protect yourself by including an option for you to end the contract for any reason by stating that you may terminate the contract at will.

7. Your signature and the signatures of all appropriate parent(s) or guardian(s).

To prevent families from leaving while they owe money, require payment at least one week in advance. If a family is unable to pay the final payment all at once, outline a payment schedule where you receive a little each week until you are paid in full. Clear and enforceable agreements are key to a successful business.

Information and sample forms are available on NAFCC's website (www.nafcc.org/effective -contract-and-policy-points). Sample contract forms may be available online from your state child care resource and referral agency or Department of Human Services. It is important to check your state licensing regulations to be sure you include all required information. In addition, federal laws prohibit discrimination on the basis of race, color, gender, religion, age, disability, or national origin.

For each family, provide written expectations and a contract signed by both parties to make sure that legal responsibilities are clearly presented and understood. You and the child's family should each keep a copy of the signed contract.

Handbook

Create a handbook for families that describes your expectations for them and what you provide for their children. Include a page in the contract that states that parents have read the handbook completely—and have them sign the statement. When you set clear terms in the contract and rules and responsibilities in the handbook, you can enforce what has been stated and signed and minimize misunderstandings.

Program philosophy and goals. An important purpose of the handbook is to create a sense of identity by sharing your goals for children. You may state your commitment to promoting children's development and learning and ensuring their well-being and safety. You may highlight open communication with families and how you use positive guidance with children, as well as other features of your unique approach.

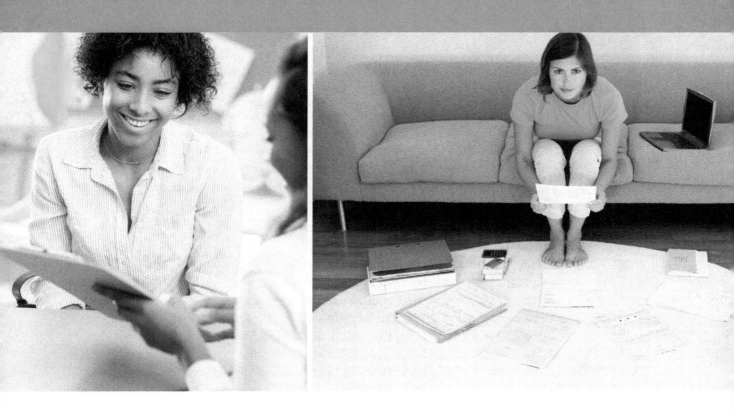

Times and days of operation. In your handbook, contract, and elsewhere, clearly state daily opening and closing times. Your own family needs to know when children will arrive in the morning and when they can resume use of the home at the end of the day. Since personal family time is also a priority, be consistent about enforcing arrival and pickup times. If there are certain days when you can make exceptions, you may include some long days. For example, you may decide that on Friday, you will extend your normal closing time by one hour. Be sure to charge overtime to discourage late pickups. Keeping a set schedule—and reinforcing it with families—allows them to better balance home and work responsibilities.

Health, illness, and safety procedures. Post written policies that outline requirements and regulations for health, illness, and safety procedures in a prominent place. These may be guided or determined by licensing standards, but there may be additional guidelines that make sense for your home, community, or climate, such as providing and using sunscreen or outerwear. Ask families to complete a written form that details each child's allergies, special needs, health issues, and changes in the family, such as a new baby, an illness, or a divorce. Sample forms are available from your state and city licensing agencies. Periodically, ask families to verify the accuracy of their emergency contact information and other medical information. In addition to including illness and attendance guidelines in your handbook, post the guidelines where families can see them. Let families know how you will handle each child's personal care routines such as diapering and toileting. Include this information in your handbook.

Contact information. Let families know how to contact you both during and after business hours. Set clear times during which you will accept calls and respond to emails.

Payments and charges. Enforce payment schedules and additional charges for overtime care in a uniform manner. Typical charges may vary by community or state, so set fees that are consistent with those in your area. Require written permission for anyone to pick up a child other than that child's parent or guardian. Make it clear that you need to receive special requests and all changes to a child's schedule, including vacations, in writing to avoid misunderstandings.

Risk Management

In addition to the handbook, keep written policies for risk management in a binder. These include emergency procedures that describe what to do during a fire, a weather event such as a tornado, a power outage, or other emergency. Risk management policies also include procedures for daily sign-in and pickup of children, health and licensing information, and annual servicing of safety equipment. Safety guidelines (such as for field trips, walks, and other outdoor experiences) and medical information (such as accident reports, CPR certifications, and child abuse trainings) should be included in your risk management binder. Review all risk management policies annually to be sure everything is up to date.

Summary

Strengthening your business practices pays off in multiple ways, including how to

» Clearly communicate expectations and responsibilities with families

» Feel confident in day-to-day operations

» Be more effective at record keeping and fiscal management

» Save time by organizing your physical space and records

» Feel confident knowing how you have addressed safety, emergency, and legal requirements

Over time, knowing where to find answers and how to get the support you need increases your knowledge and effectiveness. As a business owner, you build a strong foundation for your high-quality program by developing excellent administrative practices.

3 Learning Spaces in Family Child Care

At 5:45 p.m., the last child is picked up. Marnie quickly slides the bins of toys under the shelf by the sofa and places the basket of books by the window. She rolls the block and puzzle cart back to the laundry room, where it fits perfectly next to the dryer. Finally, she shifts the table away from the wall and replaces two chairs. She notices that the file of billing records is on the counter, so she puts them where they belong—in the locked box on the wall shelf above her desk. When Marnie's teenage daughters come in, they know that the children have already left for the day.

Making the Most of Dual-Use Spaces

When entering a family child care home, while you are able to tell that the home operates as a child care program, it also looks and feels like any other home where children live. You may have a space for written communication with families near the entry door and clipboards with sign-in sheets and notices on hooks in the hallway or on a counter or table. You might use a dresser as a communication counter, with a separate drawer for each child to store personal items, clothes, and belongings. After hours and on weekends, you can clear the top of the dresser and close the drawers to use it as a surface for your own family's use.

Furniture. Look for furniture that can be used in more than one way or easily moved when children are not present. Children can use sturdy, low coffee tables in the living room during the day. Store child-size stacking chairs in a closet or alcove at the end of the day. Many providers use child-size tables for children's play and for meals and snacks, while others use highchairs or booster seats at a dining room or kitchen table. Older children may use a dining room or kitchen table to play with small toys, create art projects, write in journals, or do homework away from ever-curious infants and toddlers.

Storage. Because your child care home may include children of a wide range of ages, to keep everyone safe, you must evaluate materials that may be safe for one age but not for another. With a multiage group of children playing together, there will be some toys and materials that are too fragile or small for infants and toddlers to use. Place these materials in clear, stackable containers and label each with the name of the material and a photo of the contents. Store them out of reach of the youngest children but where the older children can reach them. Stackable bins are easy to move or cover at the end of the day. Use open, low shelves that are secured to the wall and stable to hold baskets, portable crates, or tubs that store toys and materials for younger children.

Outdoors. Store outdoor equipment in a safe place after the children have left for the day. Place hoops and scooters in a shed or garage and other items such as balls, buckets, and shovels in plastic storage bins. Open gates that you closed and locked during the day while caring for children so that your family can access your outdoor space. At regular intervals, check your swings and climbing equipment to make sure they are safe. Maintain and repair all outdoor equipment so it is safe for children to use. Repair cracks, rusting, or splintering due to weather exposure. Remove and replace needed items. Review repair and maintenance guidelines for your state and locality for more information. Use extra caution and vigilance if the children and your family use the same space. For example, put away and secure all family gardening and lawn supplies after using them.

You need to patiently practice these routines to become skilled at serving the needs of a multiage group of children in spaces that both the children and your family use. Planned activities may not work out exactly as intended if children are tired or show a preference for something else. Thinking flexibly and respecting the children's needs goes a long way toward ensuring success. Think creatively about how to organize your space, storage, and materials. Make small changes that have big impact, such as rearranging a room to provide ample play space, providing soft pillows or beanbags on the floor for reading, and separating noisy play materials from quiet play materials. Over time, you will learn what works best for children in the unique spaces of your home. It helps to reflect about what works well and to think about how to improve your practice.

At Annaka's program, the sewing bin is one of the children's favorite activities. Annaka talks with the children as they play with sewing materials. To 5-year-old Gabriella, she says, "Thanks for your help, Gabriella. I had been meaning to untangle those ribbons, and I am so happy you worked hard to separate them." To 3-year-old Jacob, Annaka says, "Okay, I will keep this steady." She holds a piece of green felt steady so Jacob can use two hands to maneuver the fat handles of the pinking scissors. They watch the zigzag lines appear and talk about how that keeps the fabric from raveling. Next to them, 4-year-old Janna is happily stringing large beads on a cord. "I love to see the color patterns you string together," Annaka says. "My grandmother let me play with her buttons and ribbons when I was a little girl."

Annaka shares her passion for sewing, fabrics, and creativity by encouraging children to experiment with different materials. They explore the tools and fabrics that Annaka offers and then decide how they would like to use the materials. She knows the older children can handle more precise work, but she makes sure the younger ones successfully use the materials and tools that she has set out for them. Annaka understands each child's developmental needs and offers the support each one needs to learn and develop. The result is that all the children learn new skills and feel proud of their work.

Annaka is using developmentally appropriate practice, which is grounded in research that shows how young children best develop and learn. It is designed to help teachers apply their understanding of how children learn best, taking into account each child's family, language, and culture and then using that information to teach children in ways that invite motivation and engagement (Copple & Bredekamp 2009).

Voice of family child care—It means a lot to me that I can support children in ways that respect their natural strengths and their need for movement and flexibility. I am able to follow their interests and give extended time for play or take an afternoon for a building project or art activity. The children are able to rest and pursue quiet activities when they need a break. Best of all, they are always learning from each other. They often work together to investigate the yard outside or to work on a puzzle. The older children read to the younger ones. I enjoy supporting the children and love to see them so excited about discovering new things. I see amazing growth in their development over the months and years.

Keeping Safety in Mind

Nola says, "Do you have the books you want, Diego? Your camp is almost all set up. Here are the flashlights." Nola helps Diego and Flora, two 4-year-olds, place netting over a card table to make a fort and places a large dining room chair next to the card table. Julian, who is also 4 years old, crawls under the table and pulls in a pillow, a blanket, and a basket. He accidently pulls the netting, and it starts to slide off. Julian rolls over and yells, "Hey, look out, guys, the roof is falling in!" Nola quickly secures the netting and then helps Julian arrange the blanket, pillow, and books inside the cozy space. The 4-year-olds settle in and turn on the flashlights.

Nola encourages the children's idea to build a tent. She knows they need her support, so she stays nearby to watch their progress and to be available if they need help. Even though they move furniture that will need to be put back later, she knows they are going to have fun in their "camp." She wants the children to try new experiences, learn by trial and error, and to cooperate as they solve problems together. She closes the drapes to make it darker in the room and in their tent, and the children enjoy looking at books by flashlight.

A safety review is part of your daily routine. The following are a few strategies that you can use to ensure children's safety:

» Check the children's indoor and outdoor learning environment each day.

» Place items that the children should not touch out of their reach.

» Cover all electrical outlets.

» Secure and keep all cords and strings out of the way.

» Store dangerous substances out of children's reach and in a locked cabinet or container.

» Secure shelves and tall furniture so they cannot tip over or become a danger to young children.

Include in your safety review any additional strategies that make your home safe for children and that meet state and local regulations.

Evaluate the indoor and outdoor toys, equipment, and materials in your home to find and set aside any that need regular cleaning or repairing. Be sure to store materials and toys out of the reach of children who are not yet able to safely use them. Portable gates can be used for the following:

» To block off dangerous or private areas, such as a shower stall or stairs

» Between the kitchen and the living or dining room to create a safe space for children to play while you prepare lunch

» To create "infant-only" spaces near older children's active play area

(*Note:* Follow manufacturers' directions to secure gates; children must be supervised at all times.)

Because there are older and younger children moving and playing, you have many opportunities to teach children to become aware and respectful of each other. Help them understand that they are responsible for their actions, and model how to care for others by keeping a positive attitude and reminding children to watch out for others.

When safety issues arise, it is tempting to tell children to stop: "Jaden, stop tipping back in the chair. You are going to fall over and hurt yourself." To help children recognize and correct their own actions, use simple language to draw attention to what needs to be done: "It's time for a feet check. We keep our feet on the floor so that we are safe." Rather than saying "Look out! You are going to bump into Hailey!" help children learn to look for and respond to the needs of others: "Look to see where our friends are, so we can walk around them."

Giving positive feedback about safety is an effective strategy: "You were so careful when you put your plate on the counter," or "You held hands when we walked to get the mail. This helped keep us safe." Talk with the children about what is expected: "How should we hold hands to get the mail?" or "What will we do with our plates after lunch?" Focusing on strategies in positive ways helps children feel proud of what they can do to contribute to everyone's safety.

The most important aspect of safety is setting consistent expectations. Review and practice what you want children to do. Set clear limits, especially when they are nonnegotiable: "Go down the slide feet first," or "Use the chess set at the kitchen table." You can help children abide by safety rules by being consistent with follow-through. Talk with families about your expectations and ask them to support similar rules at home. Ask the children's families about the safety rules they have at home so you can support those rules when the children are with you. When you work with their families, children understand what is expected and know what the safety rules are.

An Environment that Supports Children's Learning

Three-year-old Mia lugs a backpack across the floor. Her 4-year-old sister, Nora, pulls a travel bag on wheels. The backpack and travel bag are stuffed with clothes from the dramatic play area and food from the play kitchen. "Where are you going?" asks Tamara. "We are going to visit Grandma," they respond. "Did you pack your toothbrushes and pajamas? Do you need a snack for the plane ride?" The children join Tamara in the kitchen to put crackers and cheese into baggies. In the "airplane" Mia and Nora made from cardboard boxes, the girls fasten their seatbelts and munch happily on the crackers. They talk excitedly and point to *My First Airplane Ride*, a picture book about flying to visit Grandma.

While Tamara is helping the girls on their plane ride, she is also in the middle of fixing a bottle for a young infant who is hungry and needs to eat right away. An older infant is crawling to the other room and needs to be steered back to the play area. A toddler is figuring out how to open and close the trash can. There will be days when you feel that you need extra arms and legs to keep up. Preschoolers enjoy constructing tents and forts; stacking, building, and playing with beanbags, blocks, and other materials; and playing with vehicles. They are beginning to solve problems and are creative and always enthusiastic about dress-up and dramatic play. School-age children ask big questions and are trying to figure out the world around them. Some love to read or look at books; others need time and space to construct art projects, jump and run, and explore hobbies. They may be interested in learning new games and using materials in creative ways.

To meet the diverse needs of a multiage group of children, include multipurpose, adaptive play materials in your environment. For example, instead of plastic "food" that can be used only one way, put dominoes or large wooden beads in a basket that can be used for "cooking," playing games, or many other play scenarios. You do not need expensive store-bought toys; you can use materials you have on hand to create play opportunities. Children may want to make menus with paper and nontoxic markers, play with wallets and tote bags, and use old receipt books and empty food containers to make a store or restaurant. They will enjoy exploring loose parts and building materials and sorting collections of clothespins, spools, cups, or spoons. Old road maps and a small suitcase, with child-made "passports," can inspire travel play; large boxes and cartons become boats, canoes, cars, castles, or trains that take children to places near and far. Adding music that reflects the children's languages and cultures and reading books about children around the world can open the door to new interests and ideas. Open-ended materials like these invite children's creativity and engagement.

Office supplies are great play materials. Graph paper, rulers, measuring tape, clipboards, calculators, scales, and pencils can invite math play. Board games, card games, dominoes, and sorting, matching, and stacking games promote cooperation and learning. Tools, large nuts and bolts, and old phones and small appliances (with cords and plugs removed) that children can take apart spark children's interest in learning how things work. Cotton scarves can serve as sorting mats or carrying pouches. Children can use scarves and pieces of cloth to create dress-up clothes for dramatic play. Include materials that ignite children's imagination and inspire their purposeful play.

Children with Disabilities

If you have a child with a disability in your group, ask the family to help you understand all you can about that child and his strengths and needs. You may need to modify spaces, time, or materials for some children. The child's family is your best resource. They know what works best and can suggest changes so their child has positive, successful experiences in your family child care home. Additional resources are often available in the local community and from national organizations, including

- Zero to Three offers a variety of early intervention resources: www.zerotothree.org/policy-and -advocacy/early-intervention-policy

- The Early Childhood Technical Assistance Center provides guidance about the most effective ways to improve the learning and development outcomes for young children, birth through 5 years of age, who have or are at risk for developmental delays or disabilities. The information supports children's success in inclusive settings and natural environments and addresses cultural, linguistic, and ability diversity: www.ectacenter.org/topics /earlylearn/earlylearn.asp

- The Division of Early Childhood of the Council for Exceptional Children offers information and resources for families and teachers of young children (birth to age 8) with disabilities and other special needs: www.dec-sped.org

- National Association for the Education of Young Children offers resources for supporting children with disabilities: NAEYC.org/search/disabilities

- Center for Parent Information and Resources lists early intervention resources by state: www .parentcenterhub.org/find-your-center

- National Center for Learning Disabilities provides information about laws and resources for families and professionals: www.ncld.org

- National Alliance on Mental Illness offers information and support for child mental health: www.nami.org

- National Organization on Disability is an advocacy organization that promotes the full participation of people with disabilities in all aspects of life: www .nod.org

Learning in outdoor spaces. Outdoors is a great place for science and nature exploration. Use a blanket or picnic table to host art activities or dramatic play. Inspire children's interest in local wildlife with a birdbath or bird feeder, which needs to be refilled regularly in order to attract birds. Small container gardens engage children in growing a salad garden or flowers. Children enjoy catching bugs or caterpillars, making a butterfly garden, and discovering animal tracks. Resources for more ideas about outdoor learning include these:

> » National Audubon Society's educational activities for children: www.audubon.org/get-outside/activities

> » National Geographic Kids offers a wide variety of learning resources: www.kids.nationalgeographic.com

> » National Wildlife Federation offers gardening ideas: www.nwf.org/Garden-for-Wildlife/Create/At-Home/Kids-Garden-for-Wildlife

> » National Wildlife Federation's Ranger Rick page offers activities and exploration: www.rangerrick.org

Active play. The activities you plan, such as setting up an obstacle course or making a train, can be inexpensive and use commonly available materials like baskets, balled-up socks for balls, and small and large boxes. Give children opportunities for inside and outside active play. Active play provides exercise, social fun, and self-expression. Physical activity promotes healthy weight, sleep, and appetite, and is essential as children learn to balance and coordinate their bodies (Lu & Montague 2016). Children develop social skills through active games and increase self-regulation as they learn to stop, start, and control their bodies and coordinate their movements with others (Becker et al. 2014). The American Academy of Pediatrics (AAP 2018a; AAP 2018b) recommends a minimum of two hours a day of active physical play for toddlers and preschoolers.

Plan active, physical games every week and especially on days when outdoor play is not possible due to weather. Use masking tape or chalk to mark off areas for relay games, jump rope, bowling, exercise, dance, hopscotch, and beanbag toss games. Children can take turns tossing beanbags or balled-up socks into a laundry basket or play a group game such as Follow the Leader or Freeze Dance, which can help them learn how to follow instructions and work together.

Materials for Exploring and Learning

The children scramble up to the picnic table on a warm spring day. Maria gives each child a shoebox to fill with items from the yard. Four-year-old Adnan fills his box with sticky pinecones and leaves. Five-year-old Drake sorts through the small pebbles next to the garden bed and fills his box with flat stones. Four-year-old Claudia adds a soft bed of grass and some sticks to her box. One stick has a furry caterpillar attached. Maria says, "Look what we have here! A caterpillar! I wonder if it will make a cocoon."

The children watch the caterpillar inch up the stick and then talk about the best place for the caterpillar to make a cocoon. They decide to put the caterpillar in a safe place in the yard. They look at their collections with magnifying glasses and describe what they notice about each one.

Some of the most important learning comes through teachable moments and daily activities involving conversation and shared experiences. Build on children's interests by answering questions and extending their thinking. While outside on a walk, engage children in lively conversations about the world around them with statements or questions like "I wonder if . . . ," "Why do . . .," and "What do you notice?" Give children opportunities to talk about and share what they know. Like the children in Maria's yard, you have the opportunity to explore, work together, and investigate what you find outdoors.

Selecting Materials

Basic planning can make a big difference in the way children engage with materials. Make materials such as blocks, dolls, fabric, balls, markers, and paper available every day, and offer other items, such as games, puzzles, table toys, and interesting building materials in rotation. Select materials that children can explore at their own pace and time. Store these materials in tubs, baskets, or containers that can be moved to different locations so children can use them independently or with other children in cooperative play.

Natural and found materials. Use natural and found materials such as smooth stones, pinecones, small sticks, buttons, or pieces of felt or fabric to inspire hours of creativity and exploration. Children do not need expensive toys to engage their curiosity. Tell families and friends what you are looking for, so they can add materials to your collections.

Books. Focus on reading every day to help foster children's passion for and love of reading. Set up soft, cozy spaces for curling up, reading, and private play. Place pillows on a carpet or add a basket of books and a blanket on the couch. Older children can look at picture books or read simple stories to younger children. Read books to children, including infants, daily. Point to pictures and describe what you see. Many children enjoy informational books that show how things are made or cookbooks with pictures. Some older children love to use interactive maps, do mazes, or work on puzzle books. Ask a librarian to help you locate books about topics that relate to your curriculum plan, such as STEM, getting along with others, or shapes; topics that the children are interested in such as pets, families, or funny stories; or books about the children's experiences with animals, neighborhoods, or friends. Many children also enjoy books that show how children around the world live.

Expand stories beyond the covers of the book. Provide a basket of puppets, hats, or other clothing that relates to stories that you are reading to children or that they are reading independently. Set up art materials that relate to the books you are reading to extend children's learning and imagination. Children love to read by flashlight and to use old magazines and calendars to make collages, mobiles, and weavings when they are old enough to manipulate the materials successfully.

Discovery. Math and science are part of everyday life. Talking about math and science means having conversations about concepts like *more* or *less*, *smaller* or *larger* and asking children to explain how they figured something out. Learning can be informal yet purposeful. Children enjoy solving practical problems, such as figuring out how many bananas are needed to feed everyone at snack time. Some children like to figure out how to tell time, how to count all the beads in a basket, or whether an ice cube that is in a bowl in the kitchen will melt faster or slower than an ice cube in a bowl that is outside. Include math and science materials such as a calculator, measuring tape, scales to weigh objects, and play money in the dramatic play area. Include tabletop math activities such as dominoes, card games, and magnetic shape tiles, as well as books about science concepts such as *A Fruit Is a Suitcase for Seeds*, by Jean Richards; *Water Is Water: A Book About the Water Cycle*, by Miranda Paul; or *What Do Wheels Do All Day?*, by April Jones Prince. Children enjoy using shape stencils and geoboards with pegs and rubber bands and doing tangram activities, where they copy patterns or create objects using smaller shapes. Board games encourage children to count, sort, and take turns, all of which build an understanding of mathematics concepts. When you take children on nature study walks, collect leaves, bark, pebbles, pinecones, or other natural materials that children can examine or sort. Use a notebook as a science journal or as an architect's planning book for designing block structures.

Art. Provide a variety of materials so children can choose what they want to use to create artworks that represent their own ideas and imagination. Use a plastic shower curtain or tablecloth to cover a low table so children can stand or sit to work on projects. For a change of pace, bring art materials outdoors and encourage children to let nature inspire them to draw or paint.

Children can use crayons, paints, pencils, and paper to write letters or poems or create paintings or drawings. They can use scrap paper, old magazines, fabrics, and glue in collages, mobiles, and sculptures. When children twist, glue, cut, and form the materials, they practice fine motor skills and develop creativity. Children can use paper towel tubes, washed plastic yogurt containers, small boxes, and cartons to design bird feeders or sculptures or as painting surfaces. Children can use clay and homemade playdough to make sculptures, for pretend cooking, and as a building material. Let children freely express themselves using a wide variety of art materials. Create art smocks for children from large shirts to keep their clothing clean. Cut sleeves to the appropriate length and put the shirts on over the children's clothing with the buttons in the back.

Dramatic play. Offer children the chance to understand their world and learn how to get along with others through dramatic play. All you need is a box of props and dress-up clothing. Include materials that relate to the children's experiences and interests and to your curriculum plans, such as pet care, careers (firefighter, doctor, veterinarian, police officer), camping (backpack, flashlight, binoculars, fishing equipment), travel (beach towel, camera, wallet, sunglasses), restaurant or market, birthday party, gardening, school supplies, car repair, banking, or baking. Store like items together; label each container.

Children enjoy acting out books they have read or heard, or pretending to go on a trip to the zoo or to a fire station. Have children role-play cooking or going to the store. Imitating what they have seen adults do and acting out things that happen in their world helps children understand experiences they have had. As they play, they learn to make a plan and work with others to carry out the plan. Learning is a natural part of children's exploration and play.

Share your passions. If you are passionate about cooking, art, gardening, or woodworking, let the children know about your interests so they can learn from you. You may be a whiz at handcrafts such as sewing or knitting, or you might want to share your collection of teddy bears or shells with the children.

Healthy Practices for Children

Use the following information as inspiration and practical support to create a healthy setting for children. Of course, what you decide to do depends on the needs and abilities of the children in your care.

- HealthyChildren.org, from the American Academy of Pediatrics, provides tips and information on fitness, sleep, nutrition, and health. It also includes specific guidance for children, from infants through grade school: www.healthychildren.org

- Let's Move! encourages physical health and healthy eating: https://letsmove .obamawhitehouse.archives.gov

- Nibbles for Health is sponsored by the US Department of Agriculture's Food and Nutrition services. It features healthy ideas for meals, snacks, allergies, gardening, and cold and warm weather fun: www.fns.usda.gov /tn/nibbles-health-nutrition -newsletters-parents-young-children

Health and Fitness

Four 6-year-olds set up two boxes as base to play a game of tag in the yard. "If you are inside the box, you are safe. If you are running, you can be caught," Dylan says. "I'm it!" He begins to chase the others. "No, no! I am safe. I was touching the box," hollers Maya. They play tag until they are so tired they can hardly run.

One of the greatest benefits of family child care is that children have the time and opportunity to enjoy playing outdoors. Working together, they make up rules for games, talk (and sometimes argue) until everyone agrees to the rules, and have fun until they run out of breath. Active aerobic play like this is essential to good health.

Health and nutrition affect children's daily mood and energy. They need plenty of time for fresh air, exercise, and rest every day.

Use what you know about health and nutrition to guide your daily decisions about activities and meals; check out the resources in the sidebar on page 29 for more guidance. Work closely with families to adjust routines to meet children's individual needs. Use self-care routines, such as handwashing and times for rest and sleep, to teach healthy habits and good self-care skills.

Summary

Spaces and materials inside and outside your home create a meaningful setting for relationships, activities, and learning. With planning and creativity, you organize what you have on hand and introduce new materials for exploration and play. You get to know children well and follow their interests and ideas. They show you what they have discovered and ask questions about how things work. They ask you to read books that interest them, help them figure out a puzzle, or tell you a new way to play a game. Families are eager to hear about your daily activities and the things their children are learning. You create positive learning experiences for children by thoughtfully preparing your spaces.

4 Teaching in Family Child Care

"Did you get a new toothbrush?" Renee is talking with Jayden and Isobel while they are in the bathroom after breakfast. When Isobel's father brought her in today, she was wearing pajamas, so Renee says to Isobel, "I'll help you change into play clothes." Renee helps Isobel pull on her jeans as Jayden heads for the LEGO blocks so he can play while he waits for his turn to brush his teeth. He knows how to get them by himself, because the toys are easy to access. When Jayden and Isobel finish brushing their teeth, they join the other children who have finished brushing their teeth and are playing with the dress-up clothes.

Routines and Schedules

In addition to organizing your home environment so the children's possessions and learning equipment and materials are in easy-to-access locations, set up clear routines and schedules to help your family child care program run smoothly. The routines and schedules should be flexible so you can respond to the children's needs and interests. Evaluate and adjust your routines and schedules periodically to make sure you are meeting the children's needs and effectively organizing the day.

When you have a regular daily routine and basic schedule for indoor and outdoor play, group times, meals, and rest, children know what comes next in the day, which helps them feel safe and secure. A written schedule (see the example on page 32) helps you remain flexible yet keep a basic structure for the day. You may have scheduled indoor play, but a warm, sunny morning may invite outdoor play. You may extend active play when children are organizing games, busy gardening, or enjoying gross motor equipment. At times you can move indoor play to an outdoor blanket or fort or introduce an art activity on your porch when a change of setting suits a particular activity. While you want to infuse your day with interesting projects, learning opportunities, and conversation, you can maximize the benefit of your home setting by following children's interests, engagement, and contentment level.

An Example of a Flexible Daily Schedule

6:30–8:30 a.m.: Arrival, quiet play, family-style breakfast, and self-care. Prepare breakfast before children arrive so that you can give your full attention to arriving families. Have books, puzzles, and quiet play activities available. After breakfast clean-up, flexible personal care routines including hand washing, tooth brushing, and toileting meet individual children's needs.

8:30–10:00 a.m.: Choice time activities include group games, blocks and construction play, art activities, dramatic play, reading and writing materials, fine motor and learning activities, and music and movement experiences.

10:00 a.m.: Snack time. All meals and snacks include supportive, personal conversation. Children participate in preparation and cleanup as part of a relaxed and positive routine.

10:15–11:15 a.m.: Preparation and outdoor play. Personal care routines include toileting needs and dressing in outdoor clothing and are followed by active outdoor play or a walk.

11:15–11:45 a.m.: Choice time indoor activities include shared reading, puppets, songs, and games.

11:45–12:00 noon: Cleanup and preparation for lunch.

12:00–12:30 p.m.: Family-style lunch includes talking about morning activities, personal conversation, and responsive support for developing coordination and feeding skills.

12:30–12:45 pm: Transition to nap or rest time activities includes self-care routines, quiet reading, and soothing music.

12:45–2:45 p.m.: Rest time. Older children may engage in quiet activities during this time.

2:45–3:15 p.m.: Transitional and flexible indoor play and snack. Prepare for outdoor play.

3:15–4:00 p.m.: Outdoor active play. During this time, school-age children may join you and parents may come to pick up their children.

4:00–6:00 p.m.: Choice time activities should include a wide variety of art and writing materials, age-appropriate book reading, dramatic play, and fine motor and block activities. Tailor self-care activities to the individual children during this time. Families pick up their children during this block of time.

Consistency is the key to success. If children are allowed to drop their coats on the floor sometimes but you ask them to hang them up other times, they learn that it's okay to follow through only when you ask them to do something. Children feel secure when there are consistent routines. They need to know that things like nap time happen at the same time and in the same way each day.

Arrival. During arrival time, greet the children and their families warmly and have a clear routine for putting personal items away. Have materials and books available for children to explore while you greet and connect with their families.

Personal care routines. Offer calm, sensitive support during diapering and toileting, brushing teeth, naptime routines, and other self-care routines to help children feel secure and cared for. Your positive interactions with children during self-care show them how to take good care of themselves and model how to respect others' needs and feelings. Establish happy and calm personal health routines to boost the children's self-esteem and help them develop self-care routines for a healthy future (La Paro & Gloeckler 2016; Masterson 2018).

Jobs. During the day, children can do jobs such as cleaning up play spaces, setting the table, putting on outdoor clothing, and assisting younger children. Helping instills responsibility and increases empathy and caring (Masterson & Kersey 2013; Paris 2015).

Mealtimes. Mealtimes are important times of day for nurturing, connection, and happy conversation. Everyone comes together for focused conversation, laughter, and discussion about activities—a time to get to know each other better. Family-style meals with calm, positive conversation are an important part of learning. Children have many reasons to say that their favorite time of day was lunch. Feeling cared for and enjoying healthy, delicious food can be one of the happiest times of the day.

Smooth, enjoyable mealtimes require thoughtful planning and organization. Younger infants need to be fed on demand, and older infants' schedules can shift, so it is important to be prepared. While you need to have bottles ready for infants in anticipation of feeding, you also need to plan in advance for older children. What will younger children be doing while you prepare meals and snacks? Allowing children to look at books or do fine motor activities such as puzzles or construction can be a great choice for this time.

You may be planning breakfast (or a morning snack), lunch, and an afternoon snack. Design a menu that rotates every two to four weeks so that you can shop more easily and let families know what you are serving. Schedule your shopping trips, which may include buying fresh items more frequently along with some items in bulk. You will need places to store dry foods, fresh foods, and bulk ingredients. Keep your receipts so you can track what you spend on food for meals, especially if you plan to apply for cash reimbursements from the Child and Adult Care Food Program. Save receipts if you plan to claim food deductions on your tax return. You may be able to use the standard meal allowance rule to claim food expenses. However, you will need to provide your daily attendance records and daily meal counts to receive reimbursements.

Daily interactions with families help you stay current with changes in their children's dietary needs or nutrition. When you have children with allergies or who require special food preparation, note these restrictions in writing and post them in the kitchen. If children must not be exposed to certain ingredients or foods, make sure there is no cross-contamination. Families of children who are vegan or who require other dietary modifications are the best source of information for how best to prepare, store, and serve these foods. If children have physical limitations or disabilities and need specific assistance with eating, talk with their families so you can make the necessary modifications.

> Cooper is counting out napkins while Hamza puts cups in place for lunch. "I have the biggest bowl!" shouts Carmen as she places a large bowl of apple slices next to the sandwiches. Maysa asks, "Did you remember the napkins?" Cooper says, "I got them!" as he brings the carefully counted pile to the table.

Children can help with each part of the meal preparation, from laying out bread slices to making a salad to measuring and adding the ingredients for a simple recipe to pressing apples through an apple corer. Use these teaching moments to talk about amounts and sizes.

Food preparation takes time. Do some preparations in the evenings, early in the morning, or on the weekends. Children enjoy setting the table and sharing family-style meals, as well as helping with cleanup activities. This is a wonderful time for them to learn about cooking, health, and nutrition as they talk with you during preparation and cooking. Older children may enjoy using children's cookbooks to select recipes or to discover creative ways to arrange food. Read books about farming or gardening so the children learn where food comes from.

Naptime. Consistent nap routines are important for infants, toddlers, and younger children. How will they transition from active play to quiet time before rest or nap? They can read books or listen to soft music. You may need to gently rub or pat the backs of some children to help them make this transition. Plan activities for older children to do while the younger children are getting ready to nap and while they are napping, such as quiet computer play, board games, or reading. After you get the younger children settled, you can help older children with a relaxing activity.

Seasonal routines. Coordinate seasonal events such as visits to the library, field trips to a museum or park, or a shared dinner with all of the children's families. Plan other family events such as a reading event or a music, crafts, or cultural heritage night. Some providers plan a spring picnic where all contribute to the meal. A unique benefit of family child care is the community among families. Doing special activities together helps children experience a sense of extended family and community that can build positive relationships and leave lasting memories.

Goodbye. Goodbye traditions at the end of the day can include special hand signs or hugs to help children transition to going home. If you encourage families to stay and talk, set up a routine for active play, such as using the swing set and running outdoors within a fenced area while parents are visiting. Be clear who is responsible for supervising the children—you or the families—if the children continue to play indoors or outdoors after their families arrive to pick them up.

> ## Child Development
>
> The following organizations have helpful information about child development:
>
> - Alliance for Childhood provides videos, news, and inspiration about childhood: www.allianceforchildhood.org
> - Center on the Developing Child at Harvard University offers helpful information about brain development and stress: https://developingchild.harvard.edu
> - Centers for Disease Control and Prevention provides great links to other useful sites: www.cdc.gov/ncbddd/childdevelopment
> - NAEYC for Families shares a wealth of practical support: NAEYC.org/our-work/for-families
> - The NAEYC Affiliate Network shows you where to get involved: NAEYC.org/get-involved/membership/affiliates
> - Zero to Three offers comprehensive resources on young children's development: www.zerotothree.org

An Effective Approach to Teaching

Your approach to teaching is what you add to well-designed indoor and outdoor spaces and routines and schedules. Using developmentally appropriate practice (DAP), you apply what you know about children and how they learn best, and you teach them in ways that invite motivation and engagement. The main components of DAP are

» Knowing about child development and how children learn

» Knowing what is individually appropriate

» Knowing what is culturally and linguistically important

You use this information to guide your everyday decisions so each child meets challenging and achievable goals (Copple & Bredekamp 2009).

Voice of family child care—I pay attention to what children say and do. I read their physical cues and recognize when they need time alone or help playing with others. I can respond effectively because I know what calms them and what helps them focus. For example, some children need additional support and lots of time when transitioning to other activities. I remember to use a strengths-based approach and give children positive feedback. I keep a clipboard to write reminders about materials to add or books about subjects that the children are interested in. I also watch children with their families. I pay attention to how they comfort their children, and I try to use the same words and approaches. Carefully observing children allows me to know what they need to learn and develop.

You observe children to notice what they know, can do, and understand, and then you use this information to evaluate what the children are doing, observe the changes over a period of time, and nurture additional learning.

You make decisions based on what you notice about individual children and what you know about how children their age develop and learn. For example, if an infant seeks comfort, you respond by holding, cuddling, hugging, and reassuring him. If a toddler is frustrated, you might describe what you see happening and encourage her to use new vocabulary to describe her feelings or learn how to get the help she needs. You might encourage children in preschool or kindergarten to talk about what happened and suggest a solution. Understanding each child's individual experience and perspective also increases your sensitivity and responsiveness to that child's needs. You support each child using what you know that child can do and encourage the use of new skills.

Because you know that infants and toddlers touch, feel, and taste everything within reach and that preschoolers are curious, active learners who are ready to run, play, and explore, you set up learning spaces so children can move freely and safely explore materials that interest them. Because you understand child development, you look for ways to incorporate active play like dance and movement both indoors and outdoors, and you encourage them to explore the environment in safe and positive ways. You also look for and are sensitive to children's need for rest and times of quiet or private play.

You notice and build on the children's interests. For example, you read them books about topics that are interesting to them and play games that they know and love. You encourage them to solve problems as part of their play or as a result of the activities you plan: "How much birdseed do we need? What can we use to pour it in the bird feeder?" and "Let's count to see how many cups of soup we need for lunch." Children are curious and want to understand why things happen the way they do. You keep in mind what they are curious about as you choose materials and plan interactions.

Learning and Developing

Three-year-old Mateo is busy driving his cars over the roads he has built with wooden blocks. Two toddlers are spinning like helicopters in the direction of Mateo's newly constructed bridge. Elise quickly steps in to guide the spinning toddlers to a safe

distance from the block roads and says, "Let's fly our helicopters over to the airport."
Then she smiles at Mateo. "You are a hardworking engineer!"

Elise knows that many 3-year-olds engage in solitary play. She anticipates the need for extra room for the younger children to spin. She knows it is important to redirect Joshua's focus away from the younger children and back to his own play as she guides the toddlers away from his block construction. By stepping in early to avert a problem, she helps the children to become more aware of each other.

The brains and bodies of young children develop over time. Two-year-olds are learning to manage their bodies and feelings and need gentle adult support to handle frustrations. They may not be able to understand how others feel or think. What they do easily one day may be frustrating to them on another day. What they can accomplish when rested and healthy may be a challenge when they are tired or sick. They need a flexible schedule and sensitivity to their changing needs.

Because young children need many opportunities to choose what to explore, you prepare your space and fill it with materials that children can use successfully and independently. While there are times that children want to draw pictures, paint, or focus on quiet play, they also need plenty of time for active movement. You balance their day with quiet and active play. When you notice they need a change of pace or begin to run, jump, or wrestle, that is a good time to shift to an outdoor activity. When they get overly excited, introduce a quiet activity such as a table game or an art project. Anticipating and responding to the need for both stimulation and rest is key.

Children need opportunities to play, to be creative, and to explore a variety of materials. Many family child care educators are experts at using play-based interactions to support and promote learning throughout the day.

Responsive Teaching

When 3-year-old Charlotte finishes her snack, she walks around the table, loses her balance, and bumps into 2-year-old Braydon, knocking him down. Raina gets on one knee, helps Braydon get up, and makes sure he is okay. Then she turns to Charlotte. "Oh, Charlotte. I am sorry you fell. Are you okay?" She points to the living room, where several dolls can be seen through the doorway. Look, the baby dolls are sad and need a hug too. Shall we give them hugs?" Both children follow her into the living room, where they rock the dolls, put them into the strollers, and pretend to walk them to the store.

When Charlotte accidentally bumps into Braydon, Raina immediately reassures them. She uses play as a bridge to help the children move beyond this emotional moment. At the same time, the nurturing behaviors of the play are comforting to the children. Because these children feel safe and secure, they recover quickly and engage in play with the other children.

Responsive teaching means that you notice when children need support. Sometimes the cues are obvious, such as when a child is crying or frustrated. But often children give subtle cues that require attention to their body language and facial expressions, especially when they are learning to use words to express themselves. When you respond in a soothing and gentle manner, it can help children move beyond the moment. In the same way, when a child shouts "Look at my truck!" you can share her excitement. "I see your truck. What is in the back? Are those puppies? Where are you taking them?" This genuine interest shows the child that you care about her interests, and it invites conversation about play.

When children need to calm down or express strong feelings, look for ways to meet those needs. If a child is upset, you may want to sit quietly together for a few minutes. Calming time should always be supportive. Teach children how to use their breath to calm down. When they are upset, remind them to use their breath to refocus their feelings and energy. When a child has extra energy, redirect her energy to constructive activities like running, jumping, or other active play. Consistent, caring responsiveness to children's thoughts, ideas, and feelings is essential in high-quality family child care.

Voice of family child care—The best part of family child care is that I am shaping the way children view themselves and each other. Our motto is, "We are kind. We are curious. We are loved." This is the foundation for how I respond to children and what I want them to believe. In teaching the children, I influence the way they feel about themselves. I want them to be capable, competent, and compassionate.

Children actually learn more in consistent, low-stress environments (Raver & Blair 2016; Schwartz-Henderson 2016). They thrive when they feel safe to explore, knowing they will be treated consistently with kindness and patience when they make mistakes, need help, or want to learn something. When encouragement and support are the norm, children can invest their full attention and emotions into play and learning. Even if they have had a stressful morning or are challenged by ongoing issues at home or in the community, your safe and caring words reassure and calm them. Active engagement and responsive teaching contribute positively to every part of children's development (Hamre et al. 2014).

Positive Guidance

Four-year-old Piper picks up a bowl of dominoes just as Simone reaches for the same container. The brief tug-of-war results in dominoes scattered all over the floor. Julia tells them, "Jackson is waiting for you at the kitchen table. He has the pirates' boat and parrots in the domino fort. How can you help each other pick up the dominoes so you can play with Jackson?" Piper and Simone forget their struggle and quickly pick up the dominoes so they can play with the pirate domino fort at the kitchen table.

Julia uses teachable moments, like the one with Piper and Simone, to create lessons that teach themselves. Piper and Simone learn that a little patience and cooperation result in enjoyable domino play at the kitchen table. Julia's approach helps the girls see for themselves the benefit of working together.

The small group setting of family child care offers many opportunities to use respectful and caring guidance. Just like Julia, you are a social and emotional coach for your own unique "team" of children. Like a coach, you want to help children understand common goals and give them many opportunities to practice new skills. You want them to learn about and care for themselves as much as for others and to solve problems in meaningful and workable ways. With support over time, positive guidance teaches children how to manage their emotions and regulate their behavior.

To help children become aware of themselves and of others, talk about what is happening, point out what others need, and describe the positive choices children make. Eventually, this approach helps children develop social and emotional competence, which encourages positive social interactions.

Because you practice responsive teaching and use positive guidance, you keep the children's social and emotional needs in mind as you make plans for the day. For example, when you plan for the children to engage in active play for part of the day, you know that they may need your assistance and support. You think ahead about whether children can handle what is expected. Some things you might consider include

» Are they too tired to focus on a complicated game?

» How will you involve all the children, or what will the younger ones do while the older children are playing hide-and-seek, four square, or jump rope?

» Would it be better to move your plans for active play outside?

» Do two children who are quietly and independently playing with blocks need more space to spread out their materials so that they don't interrupt each other's play?

Planning ahead is the first step in successfully guiding behavior. Modeling the skills you want children to use is part of positive guidance. When you are respectful, children learn that this is how to treat others. When you respond to a frustrating experience with empathetic words and patience, children see that respect and kindness matter. When your tone of voice is calm instead of angry, children see that there are positive ways to handle frustrations. When you model how to act with others, children learn that this is how to live with and treat others.

A few simple rules. Another great positive guidance strategy is to keep things simple. Rules should focus on what to do rather than what not to do. One family child care educator created three rules:

» Ask first. ("Ask one of your friends to help you do that puzzle.")

» Be kind. ("Use words and touches that are kind.")

» Stay safe. ("Walk around the swings so you are safe.")

Her caring and thoughtful guidance invites children to think about what is needed and to be responsible for their choices. Your home is unique, and it makes sense to create expectations that match what children need.

Redirection. Redirection is an effective strategy to shift children's attention and help them be successful. When the children are headed toward the garden, say, "To protect the flowers, please play with the ball on the driveway." Offer a gentle reminder when a child is painting on the table. "The paint goes on the paper." Rather than draw attention to the behavior you want to stop ("Don't go in the garden" or "Stop painting on the table"), state what needs to be done: "Balls stay on the blacktop," or "Paint goes on paper." You help children be responsible for their actions and behavior by making simple statements about what is needed.

Being proactive also means that you look ahead and anticipate what may happen. Before the children head outside, review the rules. "Where is the best place to play with the ball?" As you help the children set up paints, review helpful instructions: "When you need clean water, you can get it at the sink. Remember, keep your paint on the paper." Tailor instructions so that children can easily understand them.

Offering two ways to complete an activity successfully is a positive way for a child to learn how to make decisions. If children need to have their coats zipped on a cold day, you can say, "It's cold outside, and your coat needs to be zipped up. Do you want to zip it by yourself, or do you need my help?" Sometimes children want to do things alone, and other times they really need and want help. You can frame instructions as a choice: "It's time to come to the table. Do you want to sit on this stool or this chair?" or "It's time to put the books away. Do you want to put yours in the basket or on the shelf?"

Your beliefs about guidance practices may come from your own upbringing. Think about how you were disciplined as a child. How do you discipline your own children? What behaviors are easy for you to handle, and which ones push your buttons? Look at the way you respond to children. Punitive, harsh, or negative words are detrimental and make matters worse (Bear 2010; Colombi & Osher 2015). There is a direct link between respectful, consistent guidance and children's cooperation (Kersey & Masterson 2013). Understanding this link can help you choose to respond in positive and calm ways when children have challenging behavior.

In addition to ensuring caring and sensitive interactions, you can use the environment to assist with positive behavior outcomes. Look at the inside and outside environment from a child's perspective. Check to be sure there are enough materials for each child to participate and plenty of room to engage in active play. Some children may need help to start and maintain play activities. Watch and listen to anticipate when additional props or modeling how to work with a material can boost children's engagement during play.

Children need support during transitions. When children know the routine and the expectations, they are better able to handle changes with flexibility and good humor (Hemmeter et al. 2014). Children may need extra assistance between times of activity and rest, when routines are unexpected, or when they are tired.

Work with children to help them regulate their behavior by talking through options, helping them evaluate the choices they have and giving them plenty of encouragement. Young children need you to support them with brainstorming solutions and considering the best ways to approach problems. Help children learn to express and understand their feelings and others' feelings so they learn to identify their emotions, care for themselves and others, and help and show kindness to others.

When you interact with children in a consistent and caring manner, they learn to honor others' needs and feelings. When you are empathetic, children understand that compassion and caring are part of everyday life. When children feel your care and respect, they learn to treat others in the same way. Over time, with patient support and consistency, you will see positive changes in the way children respond and relate to each other.

Supporting Moments of Discovery

Livi plans a painting project on the kitchen table. But the children discover that blowing on the window creates a place where they can draw pictures with their fingers. They puff and blow and draw on the fogged glass. "I can draw my mommy!" "Here is a big tree." Four-year-olds Theo and Mack play tic-tac-toe. Livi stays flexible, and instead of insisting that the children do the painting project she set up, she supports the children's discovery: "The window is our paper today!" After watching the children for a few moments, she says, "Hmm, I wonder why the window gets all fogged up. Why do you think that happens?" Mack says, "It is cold." Livi says, "Yes. It is cold outside, and your breath is warm and wet! When the cold air and the warm, wet air meet, it condenses, creating a foggy patch on the window." Livi and the children decide to draw snow figures on the window and decorate them with hats and scarves.

Daily interactions in this family child care home are filled with curiosity, enjoyment, and conversation. You can see that the children genuinely enjoy being together. Spontaneous moments, like the one between Livi and the children, offer both fun and learning. Livi capitalizes on the children's curiosity, knowing that their "agenda" is the right one for them at that moment.

To identify children's strengths, develop a plan to discover their unique interests and skills. One way is to encourage a child to try a new activity. Watch what he does and says when he tries something new.

Voice of family child care—I "think aloud" with the children when problems arise, and I encourage them to come up with solutions instead of telling them how to solve the problem. If a child struggles with a puzzle, I say, "I wonder why that piece doesn't fit. Is the color of that piece the same color as this piece (pointing to a piece that is the same color)? What would happen if you turn it?" After reading a book, we talk about how the characters solve problems and what the children might do to solve the same problem.

Children learn through touching, smelling, seeing, hearing, and feeling. Some children explore their environment and express themselves through movement and dance. Other children use their creativity to set up dramatic play scenarios or to solve problems in their own unique way. Some children may have a good sense of spatial connections and enjoy solving puzzles. Others remember details and enjoy arranging items in patterns. Some children are natural storytellers or love to read. Some children have a great sense of humor and keep others laughing. Many children display a combination of these traits. Noticing and building on children's strengths requires sensitivity, respect, careful observation, and reflection as you consider the best ways to foster their learning.

One strategy is to ask open-ended questions that encourage reasoning: "How do you think that happened?," "What makes that work?," "What do you see that is different?," and "How does that make you feel?" When you discover a new experience in a book or in the neighborhood, ask, "Where have you seen this before?" Discover patterns in everyday materials such as food, pebbles, and leaves. Talk about the sequence of events—what came first, second, or third. Use questions and conversations to support children's conceptual thinking so they become active explorers and scientists, learning how to ask questions and find answers about the world around them. Talk about what the children see and what they're doing: "How many bananas are in this bunch? You're right, Grace, there are six. What did we eat yesterday that grows in bunches?," "Are all apples red, I wonder, or are there other colors too? What do you see?," and "If we double this recipe, how many cups of rice do we need?" This kind of hands-on, minds-on conversation makes learning meaningful.

Give children opportunities to use their special talents and abilities. Encourage them to explain how they whistle, show how they solve a math problem, or describe how they mimic someone's voice. Ask them to teach you a new skill, like how to braid a bracelet, or make a sandwich together. Leadership and initiative are skills that matter. Encourage children to plan an activity, make a skit, or create a dance. Take children's efforts seriously—and don't hesitate to learn new skills right along with them.

Learning in a Multiage Group

Grace is holding 10-month-old Layla when 5-year-old Max comes in with his mom. "We are having oatmeal with blueberries today, Max. I know you have been waiting for Blue Friday." Max is wearing his blue shirt. He notices the blue markers, crayons, and paper in the art area. As Max's mom and Grace talk together for a few minutes, Max sits on the floor as Grace helps Layla crawl onto his lap. Max shows Layla the teddy bears on the nearby shelf. "My teddy bear is eating *blue*berries today because this is *Blue* Friday," he happily tells Layla.

Grace loves to read. She keeps baskets of books organized by topics that reflect the children's current interests and what is happening in their families and communities. She often talks with them about what they like or want to do and then plans activities accordingly. She introduces a special event theme every other Friday, and the children look forward to something special they can do together. She observes the children when they are playing and interacting, and she uses what she learns about them to create learning experiences for them.

A unique feature of family child care is teaching and caring for children of different ages. Infants need focused interactions to help them communicate and learn language.

Toddlers need close support to explore the environment. Preschoolers thrive when you are interested in their play and provide materials for them to investigate. By early elementary school, many children have specific interests that you can support. They may enjoy building complex constructions, exploring robotics, or reading. They may be interested in a specific topic such as wildlife, horses, or dinosaurs. When children of many ages come together, the result is a lively and interactive environment that requires planning and sensitivity.

There are challenges and benefits of having multiple ages together. Older children need space and time away from younger children. They may need a quiet place to read, work on projects, or do homework. Younger children may become frustrated with activities that they cannot yet accomplish but may enjoy watching what older children are doing. Plan ahead to involve older children in more complex activities when younger children are napping and arrange your space so that children can work both separately and together.

There are benefits to having the older children help the younger ones. They learn to notice the needs of others and to be caring and empathetic. This warm connection is evident as children hug each other, play together, and enjoy each other's company. Like an extended family, children learn to get along and be patient.

Over time, you get to know the children very well. You learn which activities and daily routines—such as getting the mail, feeding the birds, or taking care of a pet—meet the developmental needs and interests of the children. They learn from each other and from you.

Strengths-Based Observation

Voice of family child care—It felt like Karina was fussy all of the time. After observing her carefully and taking notes, I realized that she really was fussy only after lunch when I was trying to get her to sleep and the older children needed my attention. This realization helped me to shift the baby's nap 30 minutes earlier and have activities prepared ahead of time for the older children. Now I am able to give Karina the attention she needs when she is tired.

Watching and listening to children are key parts of observation. As you observe children at play, interact with them at meals, and talk with them throughout the day, you notice their feelings, facial expressions, body language, and tone of voice. You may see changes in their response to routines, such as becoming upset about leaving a parent or being quieter (or more excitable) than usual. You notice when they learn and use new words and when new skills emerge or improve. Over time, you will become sensitive to and aware of changes in children's moods, words, skills, and actions.

Sometimes when you observe, you will want to formally document what you see and hear. Develop a schedule for when you will watch and write down what a child says and how she plays. Formal documentation might include

» Photos of an accomplishment, such as a block structure

» Videos of a creative dramatic play experience

» Drawings or writing samples

» A record of nap or rest times during the day

» Something interesting, new, or funny that a child has said

These formal documentations allow you to capture children's progress and share information with families.

Observation will help you understand how to support children's success. For example, if a child frequently becomes frustrated at a particular time of day, you can notice what led up to the behavior, how the child responds, and how the situation turns out. Then use that information to alter the routine, the environment, or your interactions with her. Perhaps the child needs more time, such as getting ready for naptime sooner or allowing more time during a transition. Maybe the child needs extra support with quiet conversation or alternative materials. Keeping notes about what happens before, during, and after interactions can help you be objective about understanding what is happening and develop a plan to help children be successful learners.

Use what you learn through observation to create a plan of action. You may want to change the timing of an activity by moving it to another part of the day. You may see that if you work with a child for a few minutes, she can play independently. By noticing and evaluating the impact of your interactions, you may be able to figure out what works best for each child.

Every day you have the opportunity to learn by observing children. What works best to comfort and soothe each child? How does a toddler show you that she is sleepy or hungry?

What activities seem to motivate each child? What do you notice about how the children interact that you can use to help children learn to be more caring and thoughtful?

Observation is an essential part of teaching children. Use strengths-based observation to recognize, honor, and build on their unique skills—what they can do well. The goal is to focus on strategies that build on the existing strengths and capabilities of children and foster their growth. It means seeing them as capable and vital learners as you look for ways to nurture their competence. This strengths-based approach to teaching is essential for high-quality family child care.

Observation also involves reflecting on what works and what can be improved. It incorporates the teaching approaches you use, including your tone of voice, timing, choice of words, and intensity. Your observation skills help you reflect on and be responsive and thoughtful about the guidance, activities, and routines that children need. You may improve your effectiveness by using observation and reflection intentionally.

Sharing Observations with Families

Share highlights of what you observe their children doing and saying to let families know about what children are learning, questions that they ask, or new words they say. When you share your observations with families, take brief written notes to document what was said and the date. This will help you remember the conversations you had with families and give you a record of what you shared with families and what they shared with you.

Observation helps you notice and give effective feedback to children. With an infant, you may say, "I see that you are smiling and looking at the ball. Do you see it roll?" For toddlers: "You found the block that fits! You solved the problem." For preschoolers: "You worked hard to figure out that pattern! Tell me how you did it." For a school-aged child: "How thoughtful and kind of you to help Nolan with his books." Drawing children's attention to strategies they use provides natural support for their growing strengths.

Observation increases your understanding of children. By watching carefully, you learn what they know and what they can do. You can watch to see when children are playing alone, interacting with peers, talking with adults, and participating in group activities. In this way, you can form a complete picture of each child's strengths and progress and use these positive observations to support caring communication with children and families.

The learning environment that you create is safe, nurturing, and inclusive for all children and families. You reflect on your teaching practices and approaches to make sure that you use bias-free practices that respect the strengths, languages, cultures, and values of all the children and their families.

Follow ethical practices when using observations to gather and share information on each child's skills, abilities, interests, and needs. This includes maintaining the privacy of children and their families and treating all information, observations, documentation, and records as confidential. As you grow professionally, continue to use observation to understand and learn from children. Use reflection to ensure sensitivity and responsiveness as you communicate with families. This cycle of learning and reflection will ensure respectful and genuine connections with families and support children's growth.

Communication

Lilli is a new child who is joining Tanisha's family child care program. She and her mom are meeting the other children and looking at the different spaces, materials, and toys. Tanisha welcomes Lilli and her mom when they arrive. "Hi, Lilli. Would you like to come with Nessa and me to see the butterflies?" Lilli's mom holds her daughter's hand. "Let's look at the butterfly garden with Nessa." Tanisha, Lilli, Lilli's mom, and Nessa head outside to see Tanisha's flower garden, which is filled with colorful butterflies.

Visiting a new family child care program ahead of time helps children feel comfortable and safe. The visit allows Tanisha time to give Lilli's mom information about her family child care home and for Lilli's mom to read and sign Tanisha's contract. Tanisha knows that building a trusting relationship is important right from the start.

Clear, positive communication is the foundation of a trusting relationship. Tanisha uses daily drop-off and pickup times to share positive information about each child: "I notice that Sammi has such a positive attitude. She smiles and laughs throughout the day, and if something doesn't go right she tries again" or "I have been waiting to hear more stories from Ryder. He has been telling me all about your new puppy." Encourage the children's families to use these times to share information about their children. They may want to let you know how their child is feeling, how long she slept the previous night, or about a special food they brought for him to eat or to share with the group. While brief, these times to touch base are important and helpful.

Ongoing communication. Provide ongoing communication through email, texts, a secure online communication portal, or an app to keep information flowing between you and the children's families. Use ongoing communication to

» Describe the activities for the coming week or a field trip you plan to take

» Talk about a topic that families are interested in, such as children's use of technology

» Let families know about the activities for children at the local library or community center

» Remind families that they need to send in more diapers or extra clothing for their children

At other times, you might send a specific message, such as an email to notify parents of a neighborhood visit to a park or to provide a written notice about schedule changes, meals, or snacks. You may want to send home a weekly or biweekly newsletter to share children's accomplishments or discoveries, to describe a topic that the children are investigating, or to let families know about special activities. Positive written communication builds bridges of trust

Child Care Forums and Networks

• Membership in the National Association of Family Child Care includes networking and support from other family child care educators: www.nafcc.org /membership

• Use online child care forums (such as www.daycare.com/forum) to share your experiences and chat with other providers about how they communicate with families.

• Hello is NAEYC's online forum to ask questions and have conversations about issues of interest to those in early childhood education: hello.NAEYC.org

and helps families know what to expect and how to best contribute.

Technology is a useful communication tool. You can create colorful newsletters that you hand to families or send by email. Some families prefer to hear from you by phone or text. Consider using an app like Baby Connect, Daycare Tracker Pro, Tadpoles Parent, Kaymbu, or HiMama. These apps allow you to give families real-time updates.

Daily updates. Families enjoy receiving a daily update. Attach a digital photo of their child happily engaged in an activity or record a video of a group of children that includes their child looking at books together or building a structure outside with twigs and stones. Create a private social media page and make sure that only the children's families can view what you post on the page. You can share resources with families about how children learn, how you use positive guidance, or community events of interest. You may want to create an interactive blog to share ideas and celebrate what children are learning. These updates and messages show that you understand how much families want to feel connected to their children throughout the day.

In-person meetings. In addition to informal daily interactions, set aside time to talk with individual families about their child. Before a child enrolls, meet with his family so they can ask questions and you can review your policies and expectations. When you talk with families about your program, ask them what they want to learn about immediately and what can wait until the end of the day. Ask families how they want to receive messages during work hours—by text, phone call, or email.

When children have minor incidents, such as scraping a knee or waking up crying from a bad dream, follow your state and local licensing agencies' regulations about how to notify families about the incidents.

After a child has enrolled, meet with the child's family again so they have the opportunity to address issues and ask questions. Share your agenda for the meeting with the family and ask them what they want to talk about. Use time effectively at the meeting by keeping track of the agenda and taking notes so that you and the family have a record of the conversation.

At parent meetings, begin by sharing positive observations about the child. What are the child's strengths and special abilities? These may include insightful, kind, or funny things the child said, new skills the child acquired, interesting questions the child has asked, the child's interests that you noticed, and activities that the child has enjoyed. Focusing on positive developments can help families recognize and understand their child's progress in learning and developing, getting along with others, expressing emotions, and cooperating with others in work and play.

While sharing positive information is important, the primary purpose of meeting with families, like all interactions, is to listen and learn. Ask the child's family members if there is anything they want to share about their child. Their insight may help you understand how you can support their child. When they share information, including any changes in their family, they help you understand their child better.

At times, a parent may have concerns about other children. The best plan is to listen and then say, "Thank you for telling me your concerns. I will keep an eye on this situation and continue to support your child." Keep information about another child or another family confidential and do not share it with others. If there are concerns with a particular child, note the concerns and address them with sensitivity. Sometimes children need extra support, patience, and encouragement to learn new social skills. Working together with families is vital to creating constructive solutions to challenges.

When you need to address an issue with a child's family, you can say, "Have you noticed that Emily needs support to (go to sleep, feel comfortable at meals, help with cleanup of toys, or whatever it is that the child needs) at home?" The family can share how they address the issue at home. If the issue does not happen at home, you can ask, "If Emily did need support at home, how would you handle it?" After you and the child's family identify the positive strategy you want to use, begin using it. "Why don't I try that strategy here, and you can try it at home? We can talk again in a few weeks (or the agreed-upon time frame) about how Emily responds." This cooperation results in a consistent approach for the child.

There may be times when a family raises issues about behavioral conflicts or wants to discuss problems they observe as their child interacts with other children. They may want to bring up personal or family issues. It is important to maintain professional boundaries and to refer families to other sources of support when the issues they raise relate to events outside of your family child care—this way you are working with families to best support each child.

When you meet with families, consider sharing information about library events, health care providers, early intervention, child mental health services, and other resources in the community. Collect information (brochures, a list of websites, or other sources) about city and county early childhood education enrichment programs, parks, zoos, and museums. Include resources in the family's home language. You can become an effective advocate by connecting families to a rich network of resources in your community that will enrich their involvement and secure a strong and healthy future for their children.

A positive relationship with families is essential. They are the experts who know their children best. You can ask directly what strengths and skills they want you to support. What advice can they share about their child's interests, the foods she likes to eat, how they comfort her when she is upset? What do they do to help their child take a nap? Are there recent changes at home that may influence how a child is responding or what he needs? Communicate openly with families to support a positive relationship so you can help their children learn and develop.

Relationships can be complicated. The more you seek to understand each family's viewpoint, the easier it will be to be patient and to empathize with the children's families. Take time to listen carefully. Emphasize shared goals. Let families know how much you appreciate their child and how much you value their insights. Long after they leave your family child care program, they will remember the way you cared about their child.

Summary

The most important key to successful teaching is knowing children well. Planning a set but flexible schedule helps you think about the best use of routines, activities, and spaces. You learn about children during meals, activities, and interactions, such as playing outside or reading with you. You use observation and knowledge of child development to make sure children are successful in their relationships with others and excited about exploring, discovering, and learning. You use teachable moments and rich conversations throughout the day to strengthen children's social skills, encourage children to try new activities, and help them test their skills. You learn when they need support and when they want to be independent. Throughout each day, children learn from you and from each other.

As you communicate with families, you become even more effective at understanding, guiding, and teaching children. Families become full partners in fostering children's success. Your family child care setting is a welcoming and responsive place for families and children to thrive.

5 Professional and Program Growth

Voice of family child care—Jenna and Natalie attended a training on literacy sponsored by their local community college. "At a training on literacy sponsored by our local community college, we learned that we could get a family child care credential by taking a sequence of courses and seminars. We joined a cohort at our local community college. Because we work with children who come from families with low incomes and families whose home language is Spanish, we received a small grant to help us with a literacy program that we all used."

Exploring Opportunities for Professional Growth

The teachers speaking above are passionate about helping children learn and develop and supporting their families. They also look for opportunities to develop relationships with others who share their goals. They know that learning from each other and holding each other accountable are important. When they meet, they share their goals, accomplishments, and challenges, and they provide mutual feedback and support.

Some of the greatest challenges you may face as a family child care educator include balancing your personal and professional life, setting aside time to take care of your own health and well-being, and making time for your own family. Some of your roles and responsibilities include

» Patience to care for tired children or to calm a worried parent

» Time and skills to organize your home and schedule

» Time and skills to be a manager, director, social worker, teacher, and advocate

» Strong interpersonal skills to relate to all the children and their families

Understanding how important your work is can motivate you to improve as a professional or to learn more about a specific topic. For example, you might want to take an online

Your local school district or library may partner with family child care educators to offer literacy activities through grant-funded partnerships. Check with your child care resource and referral agency (www .childcareaware.org) to find out about grants available in your state for family child care professionals.

training course in technology to support older children's interests and skills. Look for courses through your local school system, library, community college, or university extension programs. Reading a book about positive guidance may help you manage children's challenging behavior. Learning a few new skills or a new way of seeing things can help you become a more effective teacher.

Focus on one thing and make small adjustments. For example, if you want to prioritize your personal health and wellness, consider incorporating more music, movement, or dance in your weekly curriculum plans to help you be more active. Or plan engaging outdoor experiences in your yard. Find state cooperative extension programs and adult education programs at your local public school for information about, for example, how to attract butterflies and birds or how to plant a small garden. By setting new goals in one area, such as improving your personal health and wellness, you can plan new and interesting experiences for yourself and for the children in your program.

Even with a busy schedule, you can find encouragement and resources through your peers, online groups, and informal networks of providers. You can join networking groups on social media sites by searching for "family child care providers." Look for online learning communities specifically for family child care providers. You might follow a family child care blog or create a blog of your own. Helpful information can be found on the following blogs:

> » Tom Copeland's Taking Care of Business: www.tomcopelandblog.com
> » The Business of Family Child Care: www.greenfishchronicles.org
> » Feedspot links: https://blog.feedspot.com/childcare_blogs

Free resources to start a blog and share your ideas include these:

> » WordPress: www.wordpress.com
> » Wix: www.wix.com/start/blog
> » Weebly: www.weebly.com

Some in family child care have created networks to support each other. In some localities, community leaders join with child care centers, faith-based organizations, family child care programs, Head Start, and other local agencies to create awareness of the importance of high-quality early childhood experiences in school readiness (Wat & Gayl 2009). Public school administrators, city leaders, and professionals work together to highlight the importance of early childhood health and education. Early childhood professionals from different organizations may sponsor family child care roundtables to facilitate collaboration and learning. Providers meet for coffee to discuss issues and share resources. Local groups like these offer a sense of community and opportunities to share ideas and build friendships with other family child care educators. If you do not have a group like this in your community, consider starting your own family child care support network.

For additional information, see the "Professional Development" page on Collaboration for Early Childhood's website at www.collab4kids.org/ourwork/professionaldevelopment.

Locating Organizations and Resources

Voice of family child care—When I was asked to share my point of view as a family child care professional at an early childhood conference, I agreed. Since then, I have conducted trainings to share how I learned to successfully manage a business that serves children and families. I have built a great network that I use to collaborate with nonprofits and other organizations that are invested in early childhood education in my community.

You have many opportunities to grow professionally. Perhaps you want to learn about language acquisition and its relationship to how children learn to communicate. New resources and research about children who are dual language learners can boost your practices to a new level. Maybe you want to learn more about the business aspects of your work or how to more efficiently manage your time. You may want to explore more about your community and the social context of children and families as a way to build stronger partnerships with families. The following opportunities can help you continue to grow and learn as a family child care educator.

Professional Credentials

Many states offer credentials that require a certain number of professional development credit hours. Credentials are part of a career path and may provide a needed background in child development and other early childhood content. Credentials may be offered through state agencies, a state quality improvement training program, community colleges, or other organizations. The Child Development Associate (CDA) credential is a widely known national credential that is administered by the Council for Professional Recognition. Your state may offer a credential in early childhood education, administration, or family child care. If you do not have access to in-person trainings, consider online credentialing and professional development courses.

For more information on

» Child Development Associate credential, early childhood membership organizations, and training in your area, see www.cdacouncil.org

» State contacts for credentialing in individual states, see www.qrisnetwork.org/qris -state-contacts-map

» State Resource Library, see www.qrisnetwork.org/state-resource-library

National, State, and Local Organizations

National organizations provide practical information that you can use to improve your family child care program. The National Assocation for Family Child Care (NAFCC) is a national organization that also has a number of state affiliates. Its mission is to "support and leverage a nationwide network of providers and partners in expanding and promoting the power of family child care" (NAFCC 2018a): www.nafcc.org.

The National Association for the Education of Young Children (NAEYC) provides materials to support developmentally appropriate practice, including information on its website, periodicals, webinars and online courses, books, and other resources about best practices and professional learning and growth: NAEYC.org.

The Child Care Aware of America network works with more than 400 child care resource and referral agencies and local community partners to ensure that all families have access to quality, affordable child care. The mission of this organization is to increase the quality of care for all young children and to offer comprehensive training to child care professionals. They can help you with many things, including licensing requirements and information about training opportunities in your area: www.childcareaware.org.

The Early Childhood Technical Assistance (ECTA) Center is a clearinghouse for state-by-state information. It is a program of the Frank Porter Graham Child Development Institute of the University of North Carolina. ECTA's resources can help you locate needed information and learn more about the early childhood profession and the impact of enriched early learning experiences on children's development: www.ectacenter.org.

The National Black Child Development Institute (NBCDI) offers "culturally relevant resources that respond to the unique strengths and needs of Black children around issues including early childhood education, health, child welfare, literacy, and family engagement" (NBCDI 2018): www.nbcdi.org.

The National Center for Children in Poverty (NCCP) is "dedicated to promoting the economic security, health, and well-being of America's low-income families and children" (NCCP 2018). The resources on this site can help you explore and understand the dynamics and needs of the children in your community and the effects of poverty on development and find solutions to community risk factors: www.nccp.org.

Finally, local resources such as pediatric health organizations, the local library, nurse practitioners, family and child service organizations, and early intervention groups provide local connections to high-quality resources and services. Local organizations such as schools and local governments and agencies work together to make sure that all children in a community have the needed resources to succeed in school and in life.

Committing to Ethical Practices

The NAEYC Code of Ethical Conduct and Statement of Commitment establishes important guidelines for responsible decision making and behavior for early childhood educators. The Code addresses ethical responsibilities to children, their families, your colleagues, and the community, and it can help you resolve ethical dilemmas you face in your work. The core values and ideals and principles in the NAEYC Code will help guide your business and professional decisions with the highest level of professionalism and integrity. The Code outlines your responsibility to children to provide education in settings that are "safe, healthy, nurturing, and responsive for each child" (NAEYC 2011, 1). As you grow as a professional, you will have many opportunities for leadership in your community and state. The NAEYC Code of Ethical Conduct encourages you to collaborate with others to make a difference in the lives of children and families.

The NAEYC Code of Ethical Conduct and Statement of Commitment is available online at NAEYC.org/files/naeyc/file/positions/PSETH05.pdf.

In addition to your personal professional development, you have opportunities to improve the quality of the program you offer children.

National Accreditation

Voice of family child care—My goal last year was to become accredited. Achieving accreditation required a lot of hard work and dedication, but it was worth it. I wanted to develop my teaching to meet each child's individual needs, abilities, interests, language, and culture. Because I have two children in my program who each have a disability, this was a huge motivation to become accredited. I wanted to achieve the very best for them. The most surprising part was reflecting on my own practice and realizing how much each area of my work affects the children.

Operating a high-quality family child care program is a goal for many educators. Going through the accreditation process is one way to help you improve your program so you create the best learning environment and outcomes for children.

Support from NAFCC

NAFCC promotes professional development and offers support through state and local associations. It provides advocacy, training, education, and membership for family child care professionals. This includes information about the health, education, and welfare of children and the policies that affect family child care homes and the children and their families who are served by family child care. You can find more information on the NAFCC website: www.nafcc.org.

NAFCC offers a nationally recognized accreditation for family child care providers. They also have advocacy and training opportunities (NAFCC 2018b). Accreditation is a commitment to ongoing quality improvement. The first step of the accreditation process is a self-study that helps you evaluate all aspects of your program. You examine the quality of your interactions and relationships, your physical environment, and children's learning opportunities. In addition, you review your safety and health practices. Finally, you consider the effectiveness of your professional and business practices.

When you are ready, a representative from NAFCC visits and uses the organization's Quality Standards for Accreditation to give you feedback and support. The timeline for the process and additional supports and resources are available on the organization's website. Getting accredited will help you reach "a high level of quality through a process that examines all aspects of the family child care program" (NAFCC 2018b).

Nationally accredited child care homes meet the highest standards of quality for family child care. Once you are an accredited provider, your business will be listed on the national website.

Quality Rating and Improvement Systems

Voice of family child care—I was too shy to start the QRIS process myself, so my friends encouraged me to do it with them. We contacted our local early child care trainer. She showed us how to become part of our state QRIS process. It is the best thing I ever did! In addition to learning so much about myself, I have made many new friends. I have had opportunities to grow and learn and have changed so much in how I think about myself as a professional.

State quality rating and improvement systems (QRISs) provide a way for you to increase quality and receive benefits at the same time. When you participate, you can receive training, mentoring, technical assistance, and other support. There are also financial incentives, such as tiered subsidy reimbursements from the Child Care and Development Fund (CCDF), which pays a higher reimbursement rate to providers who meet standards beyond minimum licensing and who have children in their program from families who receive CCDF subsidies (www.acf.hhs.gov /occ/resource/child-care-and-development-fund).

Finally, you receive benefits when you are awarded a QRIS circle of quality or a star level. The level of quality you earn is posted on the state website so families can see your rating when they are looking for family child care settings with the highest levels of quality.

Your family child care program will be evaluated using a checklist of standards that are unique to your state. An evaluator may use an environmental early childhood rating scale that is specifically for family child care providers. As part of your involvement in the QRIS process, you will receive coaching, training, or technical assistance support that may help you improve the quality of your program. In addition, you will receive information about the family child care or early childhood credentials available to help you increase your professional knowledge and skills. The QRIS National Learning Network provides links to state resources and information, including evaluation, incentives, and professional development opportunities.

> ### Quality Rating and Improvement Systems
>
> Quality rating and improvement systems (QRISs) provide information, training, and connections to additional local and state resources:
>
> - QRIS Network State Resource Library: www.qrisnetwork.org/state-resource -library
> - QRIS State Contacts: www.qrisnetwork .org/qris-state-contacts-map
> - NAEYC QRIS Implementation: Technical Assistance: NAEYC.org/our-work/public -policy-advocacy/qris-implementation -technical-assistance

Summary

As a family child care professional, you have the opportunity to grow as a leader and enjoy the support of other early childhood educators. You can take steps to improve your own practice and explore a variety of training and credentialing opportunities. Pursuing accreditation is an important step to achieving the highest levels of quality in your work. By joining state and national early childhood organizations, you will discover a wealth of resources, conferences, and additional opportunities to develop your skills.

Finally, participating in your state QRIS will connect you to people and resources and will provide inspiration for your professional journey. You can build your qualifications and expertise and feel satisfied knowing that you are making a difference for other professionals and the families you serve. As you continue on your professional journey, you will meet many people who can help you grow as a professional and inspire and motivate you to achieve your goals.

In Conclusion

Thank you for being a family child care provider or considering becoming one. If you already care for and educate children in your home, you know how challenging *and* rewarding your work can be. Perhaps you have already pursued accreditation or participated in your state quality rating and improvement system. You already recognize that you are in the company of caring professionals who are dedicated to making a difference for children and families.

When you become a family child care educator, you join a remarkable and dedicated group of professionals who understand how to manage a business from home. You gain a network of professional support and develop friendships that will encourage and inspire you in your professional journey. As a family child care educator, you will work with others to ensure that all families can find high-quality education for their children.

With developmentally appropriate practice as the foundation of your work as an educator, you can be certain that children are receiving the support and education they need to thrive. Using your knowledge of child development, you individualize care for children, valuing and respecting their family's language, culture, and community.

With national, state, and local support, you can feel confident as you begin or embrace new opportunities for growth as a family child care professional. You will find the resources, support, and encouragement you need to begin or enhance your program. We hope the information in this book inspires a fresh vision for excellence that empowers you to meet the needs of the children and families in your family child care home.

References

AAP (American Academy of Pediatrics). 2018a. "Preschooler - Physical Activity." Accessed May 22. www.aap.org/en-us/advocacy-and-policy/aap-health-initiatives/HALF-Implementation-Guide /Age-Specific-Content/Pages/Preschooler-Physical-Activity.aspx.

AAP. 2018b. "Toddler - Physical Activity." Accessed May 22. www.aap.org/en-us/advocacy-and -policy/aap-health-initiatives/HALF-Implementation-Guide/Age-Specific-Content/Pages /Toddler-Physical-Activity.aspx.

Bear, G.G. 2010. *School Discipline and Self-Discipline: A Practical Guide to Promoting Prosocial Student Behavior*. New York: Guilford Press.

Becker, D., M. McClelland, P. Loprinzi, & S. Trost. 2014. "Physical Activity, Self-Regulation, and Early Academic Achievement in Preschool Children." *Early Education and Development* 25 (1): 56–70.

Bueno, M., L. Darling-Hammond, & D. Gonzales. 2010. "A Matter of Degrees: Preparing Teachers for the Pre-K Classroom." *Education Reform Series*. Report. Washington, DC: Pew Center on the States. www.pewtrusts.org/~/media/legacy/uploadedfiles/wwwpewtrustsorg/reports /pre-k_education/PkNEducationReformSeriesFINALpdf.pdf.

Child Care Aware of America. 2018. "Getting Your Business Licensed." Accessed May 22. www .childcareaware.org/providers/opening-a-new-child-care-program/getting-your-business -licensed.

CCRS (Child Care Resource Service, University of Illinois at Urbana-Champaign). 2009. "Child Care Provider Search." Accessed May 22. http://ccrs.illinois.edu/index.html.

Cohen, N.J. 2010. "The Impact of Language Development on the Psychosocial and Emotional Development of Young Children." In *Encyclopedia on Early Childhood Development: Language Development and Literacy*, e1–e5. QC, Canada: Centre of Excellence for Early Childhood Development & Strategic Knowledge Cluster on Early Child Development. www.child-encyclopedia.com/sites/default/files/textes-experts/en/622/the-impact-of -language-development-on-the-psychosocial-and-emotional-development-of-young-children .pdf.

Colombi, G., & D. Osher. 2015. "Advancing School Discipline Reform." *National Association of State Boards of Education Leaders,* Report Vol. 1, No. 2. Report. Arlington, VA: National Association of State Boards of Education. www.nasbe.org/wp-content/uploads/ELR _Advancing-School-Discipline-Reform.pdf.

Copple, C., & S. Bredekamp, eds. 2009. *Developmentally Appropriate Practice in Early Childhood Programs Serving Children From Birth Through Age 8*. 3rd ed. Washington, DC: NAEYC.

Denham, S.A., & C. Brown. 2010. "'Plays Nice with Others': Social-Emotional Learning and Academic Success." *Early Education and Development* 21 (5): 652–80.

Farinde-Wu, A., C.P. Glover, & N.N. Williams. 2017. "It's Not Hard Work; It's Heart Work: Strategies of Effective, Award-Winning Culturally Responsive Teachers." *Urban Review: Issues and Ideas in Public Education* 49 (2): 279–99.

Girard, L.-C., J.B. Pingault, O. Doyle, B. Falissard, & R. Tremblay. 2016. "Expressive Language and Prosocial Behaviour in Early Childhood: Longitudinal Associations in the UK Millennium Cohort Study." *European Journal of Developmental Psychology* 14 (4): 381–98.

Hamre, B., B. Hatfield, R. Pianta, & F. Jamil. 2014. "Evidence for General and Domain-Specific Elements of Teacher-Child Interactions: Associations with Preschool Children's Development." *Child Development* 85 (3): 1257–74.

Harper Browne, C. 2009. "Almost Like Family: Family Child Care." Research brief. Washington DC: Center for the Study of Social Policy. www.cssp.org/publications/neighborhood -investment/strengthening-families/top-five/almost-like-family-family-child-care -october-2009.pdf.

Head Zauche, L., T.A. Thul, A.E. Darcy Mahoney, & J.L. Stapel-Wax. 2016. "Influence of Language Nutrition on Children's Language and Cognitive Development: An Integrated Review." *Early Childhood Research Quarterly* 36 (3): 318–33.

Hemmeter, M.L., M. Ostrosky, K. Artman-Meeker, & K. Kinder. 2014. "Planning Transitions to Support All Children." *Teaching Young Children* 7 (5): 9–11.

Kemple, K.M., J. Oh, E. Kenney, & T. Smith-Bonahue. 2016. "The Power of Outdoor Play and Play in Natural Environments." *Childhood Education* 92 (6): 446–54.

Kersey, K.C., & M.L. Masterson. 2013. *101 Principles for Positive Guidance with Young Children: Creating Responsive Teachers*. Upper Saddle River, NJ: Pearson.

King, D. 2012. "Helping Children and Families Develop a Sense of Belonging." *Exchange* (208): 57–60.

La Paro, K.M., & L. Gloeckler. 2016. "The Context of Child Care for Toddlers: The 'Experience Expectable Environment.'" *Early Childhood Education Journal* 44 (2): 147–53.

Laughlin, L. 2013. "Who's Minding the Kids? Child Care Arrangements: Spring 2011." *Current Population Reports,* P70-135. Washington, DC: US Census Bureau. www.census.gov /prod/2013pubs/p70-135.pdf.

Lu, C., & B. Montague. "Move to Learn, Learn to Move: Prioritizing Physical Activity in Early Childhood Programming." *Early Childhood Education Journal* 44 (5): 409–17.

Masterson, M. 2018. *Let's Talk Toddlers: A Practical Guide to High-Quality Teaching*. St. Paul, MN: Redleaf.

Masterson, M., & K. Kersey. 2013. "Connecting Children to Kindness: Encouraging a Culture of Empathy." *Childhood Education* 89 (4): 211–16.

NAEYC. 2011. "Code of Ethical Conduct and Statement of Commitment: Supplement for Early Childhood Program Administrators." Washington, DC: NAEYC.

NAFCC (National Association of Family Child Care). 2018a. "About Us." Accessed May 22. www .nafcc.org/about-us.

NAFCC. 2018b. "Accreditation." Accessed May 22. www.nafcc.org/accreditation.

NBCDI (National Black Child Development Institute). 2018. "Who We Are." Accessed May 22. www.nbcdi.org/who-we-are.

NCCCQI (National Center on Child Care Quality Improvement) & NARA (National Association for Regulatory Administration). 2015. "Trends in Family Child Care Home Licensing Regulations and Policies for 2014," Research Brief #2. Joint research brief. Fairfax, VA: National Center on Early Childhood Quality Assurance. www.naralicensing.org/assets/docs /ChildCareLicensingStudies/2014CCStudy/fcch_licensing_trends_brief_2014.pdf.

NSECE (National Survey of Early Care and Education Project Team). 2016. "Characteristics of Home-Based Early Care and Education Providers: Initial Findings from the National Survey of Early Care and Education." Technical report of NSECE; OPRE Report #2016-13. Washington, DC: Office of Planning, Research and Evaluation, Administration for Children and Families, US Department of Health and Human Services. www.acf.hhs.gov/sites/default/files/opre /characteristics_of_home_based_early_care_and_education_toopre_032416.pdf.

Paris, B. 2015. "Hands on to Help Others: Service-Learning as a Cross-Cultural Strategy to Promote Empathy and Moral Development in the Preschool Classroom." *Childhood Education* 91 (6): 451–56.

Porter, T., & J. Bromer. 2017. "Building a Coordinated System of Support for Family Child Care: Lessons Learned from Philadelphia." *Research-to-Practice Brief*. Chicago: Erikson Institute Herr Research Center. www.erikson.edu/wp-content/uploads/Systems-Building-Practice-Brief -Porter-Bromer-2017.pdf.

Raver, C., & C. Blair. 2016. "Neuroscientific Insights: Attention, Working Memory, and Inhibitory Control." *Future of Children* 26 (2): 95–118.

Redford, J., D. Desrochers, & K. Mulvaney Hoyer. 2017. "The Years Before School: Children's Nonparental Care Arrangements from 2001–2012." *Stats in Brief*, NCES 2017-096. Washington, DC: US Department of Education, National Center for Education Statistics. https://nces.ed.gov /pubs2017/2017096.pdf.

Schwartz-Henderson, I. 2016. "Trauma-Informed Teaching and Design Strategies." *Exchange* (231): 36–40.

Vallotton, C., & C. Ayoub. 2011. "Use Your Words: The Role of Language in the Development of Toddlers' Self-Regulation." *Early Childhood Research Quarterly* 26 (2): 169–81.

Wat, A., & C. Gayl. 2009. *Beyond the School Yard: Pre-K Collaborations with Community-Based Partners*. Report. Washington, DC: Pew Center on the States. www.pewtrusts.org/~/media /legacy/uploadedfiles/pcs_assets/2009/beyondtheschoolyardpdf.pdf.

Acknowledgments

Thank you to the caring and dedicated family child care educators who shared their personal stories, insights, and reflections with us. Thank you to Kathy Charner for her encouragement and guidance in the development of this book, as well as those who provided helpful reviews.

This book is dedicated to the amazing, compassionate, and committed professionals who care for children in their homes, and who support, encourage, and work with families to prepare children for school and life. You make your communities stronger and the world a better place for children.

About the Authors

Marie L. Masterson, PhD, is director of quality assessment at McCormick Center for Early Childhood Leadership, where she oversees evaluation for Illinois' quality rating and improvement system. Marie is an educational consultant to state departments of education, schools, child care centers, and social service and parenting organizations. She is a national speaker, child behavior expert, researcher, and author of multiple books and articles that address behavior guidance, early care and education, parenting, and high-quality teaching. Marie conducts research and training on a variety of topics, including behavior guidance, raising responsible children, high-quality family child care practices, program leadership, media influences on children, resilience, and the social and emotional development of infants, toddlers, and young children. Her goal is to help caregivers, teachers, and parents understand the needs and perspectives of children. She advocates for strengths-based practices that foster resilience, especially for children who have experienced trauma and stress. She is a former Fulbright Specialist, professor of early childhood education, and early childhood specialist for the Virginia Department of Education.

Lisa M. Ginet, EdD, is the director of Erikson Institute's Early Math Collaborative. She has been an early childhood educator for more than three decades—as a classroom teacher, child care provider, parent educator, home visitor, teacher trainer, and adjunct faculty. She has worked in diverse settings, including child care centers, elementary and middle schools, a family resource agency, a family child care home, a community college, and a private university. Lisa engages children in active and meaningful learning and supports families as their children's first and closest teachers. She seeks to involve educators in reflective and practical dialogue to help improve their teaching. Her research interests lie at the intersection of theory and practice: What does it mean for a teacher/caregiver to have taught a concept or for a child to have learned it? What sort of supports help teachers/caregivers become most effective in their work with children? How do we nurture relationships among children and adults in classrooms, schools, and communities so that that all children are nurtured and challenged in safe and appropriate settings?

Printed in the USA
CPSIA information can be obtained
at www.ICGtesting.com
JSHW051457130124
55392JS00005B/9

9 781938 113352